How to Behave

Library of Congress Cataloging in Publication Number: 2011922692

ISBN: 978-1-59474-547-8

Printed in China

Typeset in Sabon, Chalet, and Trade Gothic

Designed by Doogie Horner

Production management by John J. McGurk

Quirk Books
215 Church Street
Philadelphia, PA 19106
quirkbooks.com

10 9 8 7 6 5 4 3 2 1

How to Behave

A Guide to Modern Manners

By Caroline Tiger

QUIRK BOOKS

PHILADELPHIA

CONTENTS

CHAPTER 2
AT THE OFFICE

CHAPTER 3
BIG-CITY LIVING

CHAPTER 4
LEISURE TIME

CHAPTER 5
DATING, LOVE, AND SEX

CHAPTER 6
OUT ON THE TOWN

CHAPTER 7
WHILE IN CYBERSPACE

INTRODUCTION

Have you ever been to a formal dinner and not known which fork to use? We feel for you, but *How to Behave* won't advise you on such a superficial matter—other than to ask, why are you attending such a stuffy dinner party? Tea-sipping and fork exclusivity may have been priorities for the Victorian-era leisure class, but it's all the average man or woman can do today to find time to meet a friend for a drink. And chances are you'll have to deal with several rude people on the way to that drink—on Facebook, in the subway, in a taxi, on the sidewalk, and maybe even at the bar.

In the twenty-first century, "etiquette" means something different from pinkies held at attention while sipping tea. Nowadays, etiquette is defined more by common courtesy, by showing small kindnesses to your fellow human beings during the course of everyday life. That means: No holding your rolled-up umbrella sideways so it's poking passersby; no commandeering a treadmill during your gym's rush hour for 55 minutes and then forgetting to wipe off your sweat; no joining the 10-items-or-less express line at the supermarket if your basket holds more than 10 items; no tagging photos on Facebook of friends having bad hair days; no blabbing loudly on your cell phone on a train. Nitpicky? Maybe. But necessary, because modern society enforces so few rules, and people need some guidelines to keep from being inexcusably rude.

We're lucky to no longer be bound by ludicrous flatware restrictions—today's lifestyles are much freer—but that doesn't mean people should be allowed to act rudely. In *How to Behave*, we'll give you suggestions for how to respond to a litany of abysmal behaviors typically exhibited by an endless lineup of offenders—the dreaded headrest jiggler, the armrest hog, the sweat swapper—as well as ways to spot your own bad behavior before you, too, join this army of boors.

In the pages that follow, you can take your choice of step-by-step techniques designed to correct many of the modern practices that define misbehavior. Provided stratagems range from polite to confrontational to passive-aggressive (to sometimes just plain weird). If you happen to choose a more aggressive strategy, consider yourself a warrior in the fight to end rudeness.

Why can't we all just get along? Because, alas, people aren't always nice to one another—and, if they were, there'd be no need for this book.

CHAPTER 1

PLANES, TRAINS, AND AUTOMOBILES

There's a lack of control that goes hand-in-hand with these modern machines. Do you really have any idea what's delaying the train or why you've been sitting on the runway for hours? You may have enough control over your car to express your impatience by leaning on the horn, but that's not going to get you out of gridlock traffic, is it? When people feel out of control, they may feel inclined to act out of control. But you can help break this cycle by adhering to a few basic rules of behavior.

IN FLIGHT

The constant overbooking of flights, the gruel they dare to call food, the surly flight attendants, the outrageous charges for luggage, the long waits while we're herded through extensive security checks then forced to stand by while our shoes are pulled off and X-rayed—air travel is a hassle. And nothing worsens the experience than when passengers neglect the basic rules of in-flight civility.

Armrest Decorum

The basic armrest rule is this: One to a customer, whether you're in an aisle, center, or window seat. The unclaimed center armrest is negotiable, but the center seat passenger should have first dibs—after all, this poor person is hemmed in on both sides.

What happens when you're in a cozy center seat, sandwiched between two strangers, and both the man on your left and the woman on your right are using two armrests? Are they particularly large people? No. Are they simply oblivious to your discomfort? Most likely, yes. It falls to you to point out the error of your seat companions' ways.

1. First, choose which seatmate to confront: the aisle sitter, who has to deal with people going up and down the

aisle, bumping into him? Or the window sitter, who has as little leg room as you do? It's a tough choice, but you should address the person who seems the most pleasant and approachable.

2. Once you've chosen, emit an audibly heartfelt sigh to get your seatmate's attention.

3. When she looks your way, engage her in small talk. Here are some starters: Where are you from? Are you traveling for business or pleasure? Do you know if we get a meal on this flight?

4. Attempt to create a bond with her by lamenting the inhumane conditions—including the dismal grub—of economy class.

5. Once she begins to exhibit empathy (nods of the head, sympathetic touches of your arm), gently state, "You probably didn't even realize it, but you're using two armrests. Would you mind if I used this one?"

6. Gaze at her dolefully. You may even want to briefly demonstrate for her how exceedingly difficult it is to spread out your book on your lap without the use of an armrest.

7.   Once she surrenders the armrest, thank her for her kindness and be sure to accommodate any of her wishes—within reason—during the rest of the flight.

When the Direct Approach Fails

If, after step 5, your seatmate refuses to surrender an elbow rests, you have license to be more aggressive. Simply maneuver her off the armrest with some quick elbow-to-elbow action.

1.   Plant your elbow firmly on the armrest, even if you can only fit half.

2.   By doing so, you will likely come into contact with your neighbor's elbow and/or forearm. Do not shy away from the physical confrontation.

3.   Be prepared to hold your ground. Wedging your wrist and forearm against your rib cage, actively resist the pressure of your neighbor's elbow. Think arm wrestling—but, of course, with elbows.

4.   Decisively nudge your neighbor's elbow completely off the armrest.

ETIQUETTE TIP

Improvise. Make use of props around you. Hold your in-flight beverage so that, should the armrest hog return your pressure, she risks a dousing with your Bloody Mary. (Even boors quickly recognize how unappealing it is to sit on a flight in wet clothing.)

Negotiating the Aisle

As part of their four- to six-week training program, flight attendants learn how to maneuver smoothly and efficiently up and down narrow and cramped center aisles. Passengers should take a cue from our in-flight professionals and learn to:

1. Move through the cabin with minimal jostling;

2. Take care not to hit aisle-seat passengers with bags or stray elbows as they pass;

3. Refrain from grabbing seat backs unless turbulence leaves them no alternative.

Dealing with the Incessant Jiggler

Of course, there are always those passengers who insist on bringing aboard the maximum number of carry-ons, and since one person can't successfully maneuver a purse, a backpack, and a plastic bag filled with snacks and games for their screaming baby, the sharp edge of the backpack will invariably bump up against your head and rest there as the passenger tries to stuff everything into the overhead compartment.

Then there are those who keep their balance during even the mildest turbulence by grabbing on to headrests as they hurtle down the aisle toward the bathroom, oblivious to the restful heads that are being jiggled to and fro every time they catch themselves from falling. These seat jigglers are the bane of every aisle-seat occupant. But there is a solution.

1. The next time the jiggler jiggles, quickly jump to your feet.

2. Politely capture your jiggler's attention (taking care not to touch your assailant or disturb fellow passengers) and point out the error of her ways in a friendly but firm manner: "Excuse me—you probably didn't notice, but you're jiggling my headrest each time you pass down this aisle."

3.   If she continues to stare at you blankly, point out the con-
      sequences of the jiggling: "And when you jiggle my head-
      rest, it shakes my head around [demonstrate by pretending
      you're a bobble-head doll], which is very jarring."

Ideally, the jiggler will simply apologize and move on,
taking care to move along the aisle without another jiggle. But
when a jiggler persists in jiggling, you may have to take the
following, more extreme approach. (Note: This tactic will suc-
ceed only when the jiggler is also seated in an aisle seat.)

1.   Locate the jiggler's seat by watching her as she jiggles
      her way back from the bathroom. (In larger planes with
      multiple cabins and aisles, you may need to leave your
      seat and surreptitiously tail your assailant.)

2.   Get up from your seat and amble toward the jiggler's
      row. (It helps if the theme song from *The Good, the Bad,
      and the Ugly* is playing in your head.) Keep your arms
      casually crossed over your chest.

3.   As you make your way past her seat, jut your elbow out
      at a 45-degree angle and forcefully nudge the upper cor-
      ner of the jiggler's seat.

4.   Feign nonchalance by humming or singing under your breath and looking around the cabin.

5.   As you turn and make your way back, take care to jab her seat one more time as you pass.

Observing Air Silence

When on an airplane, passengers must maintain an awareness of not only the personal space around their seat but also the sounds they may be releasing into the cabin. One person's music is another person's noise, and in a close environment like the cabin of a plane, being exposed to sounds you don't wish to hear can cause your blood pressure to rise.

According to air travel experts, this means portable listening devices should be tuned to a volume no higher than midrange. The goal is to restrict your music from floating beyond the immediate environs of your seat.

But what happens when a fellow passenger does not follow these guidelines? He may be sitting two seats away, and you can still hear the bass pumping from his laptop. Even worse, he's procured the latest album by an Artist You Hate, and you can barely get through a page of your book without being driven to distraction. How to make him aware of his transgressions without causing an ugly scene?

1.   Tap the man on the shoulder and ask him to turn down his music, please. You can hear it clearly from two seats away.

2.   Most times, your request will do the trick. But if this approach isn't successful, you may need to call in the artillery: Press the button that signals the flight attendant.

3.   When the flight attendant arrives at your seat, explain politely that you can hear this man's music even though he's listening to a "personal" stereo. She is trained to deal with passenger complaints and conflict resolution. Leave it in her capable hands.

If even this approach isn't successful, you'll need to resort to a more drastic measure that will have you singing and dancing along with the music.

1.   Place yourself directly in the offender's line of vision.

2.   Tune into his music and begin to mouth the words suggestively. (This works especially well with boy band ballads.)

3.   Like all good entertainers, make use of your hands to express such lyrics as, "Do you think I'm sexy?"—e.g.,

pointing toward him at "you," then gesturing toward yourself at "I'm sexy," and following up with an arch of the eyebrows.

4.   Groove in your chair, making sure to employ some really obnoxious dance moves, including "shopping at the supermarket," "raising the roof," or "the white man's overbite."

5.   The key to this method is to dance to the beat of the music the offender is listening to, so he recognizes that your odd behavior is linked to his own.

ETIQUETTE TIP
Cheesy dancing: The sight of a grown-up dancing cheesily in public is usually enough to shock high-volume junkies into an amazed (and perhaps even respectful) silence.

Defending against the Garrulous Seatmate

There are no rules dictating that a passenger can't talk (and talk and talk) to a fellow passenger, but common courtesy (in the air and on the ground) dictates that passengers not overstay their welcome when engaging in in-flight conversation.

Usually older, usually filled with anecdotes about her cat

or her bunion operation or her wonderful daughter or son or grandchild, the garrulous seatmate is one of the most feared— if perhaps best-intentioned—offenders in plane travel's motley lineup. You're strapped into your seat with no escape, sitting next to someone who loves to hear herself talk. What to do?

1. Grab a book, a magazine, or your smartphone. This is the obvious solution. Reach down into your carry-on and pull out whatever reading material you can find. Open wide and stick your nose in. Or if you prefer to listen to music, put in your ear buds.

2. If you're not a reader or just forgot to bring a book, remember that planes usually stock copies of their in-flight magazines in each seatback. If they forgot to stock yours, pull out the safety instructions, the barf bag— anything with words printed on it.

3. If the offender continues to spin yarns despite your being (or pretending to be) engaged in reading, say politely and firmly, "I'm sorry. I'm just really into my [book/magazine/safety card/playlist]. I don't mean to be rude, but I'd rather read/groove than talk right now." Even those who don't understand the basic social cues will get the message.

Another approach to defending against the nonstop talker involves simple one-upmanship: For every story he or she tells, you've got one that's better. Her daughter Betsy just had quadruplets? Your sister just had septuplets! And get this, she and her husband think they conceived Huey, Dewey, Louie, Pittooey, Phewey, Bill, and Sam on their second honeymoon! Oh, they had the most wonderful time. They found a great deal on a package to Maui, and . . . you get the point. (Note: For this tactic to work, you have to talk longer than your seatmate does. If her Betsy story is 5 minutes, yours has to be 15. Be obnoxious—otherwise she'll merely think she's found a companion who likes to converse as much as she does.)

Let Her Hear Your Body Talk

Body language is an effective way to send a message to a seatmate.

To convey that you're open to conversation:

1. Use sustained eye contact.
2. Smile.
3. Use friendly body language (leaning in slightly, mirroring her gestures, and so forth).

To convey that you're not open to conversation:

1. Look away or avoid eye contact.

2.   Slightly furrow your brow.
3.   Use isolating body language (slumping in chair, nose buried in book, earphones on, and the like).

ETIQUETTE TIP

Bodies talk. Wind breaks. In fact, it does so an average of 10 times a day for each of us, resulting in the release of about 120 cubic inches of gas during a 24-hour period. The longer your flight, the more likely that gas will be passed, especially if you've eaten broccoli, cabbage, or beans that day. Since only 1 in 10 farts is stinky, it's likely they'll pass undetected, unless, of course, it's a blaster. If it is detected, excuse yourself—sheepishly. And if it comes from another source, try your best to ignore it. Get up and walk around the cabin until the smell dissipates.

ON BOARD THE COMMUTER TRAIN

The average commuter train is overcrowded and under- or overheated, with hard seats and zero elbow room. With signs admonishing "No Spitting," "No Feet on Seats," "No Smoking," "No Eating," and "No Passing between Cars," you'd think commuters would be clear on all the rules. Instead, it's as if they feel these dictates stifle their self-expression, and they need to compensate by indulging in sometimes unfortunate interpersonal behavior.

It doesn't have to be this way. Whether maneuvering on the platform, attempting to carve out a small space for newspaper reading, or placing a cell-phone call, commuters have at their disposal a repertoire of survival techniques, and they don't always have to come at the cost of rude behavior.

Platform Clusters

There's always that group of people who know exactly where the door will end up once the train pulls into the station. Maybe there are three such spots; maybe there's just one. You'll know when you spy the cluster of experienced passengers huddled together, all vying for proximity to a two-foot-wide (door-width) area on the platform. Follow their lead—daily commuters won't steer you wrong. But they could indulge in bad platform behavior, like taking advantage of the inches between you and another passenger in the cluster to wedge their shopping bag in and get in front of you.

Cutting in line is the height of bad commuter form. One should not indulge in it (unless provoked), and one should always be on guard in case others attempt it. What would happen if we all started cutting in lines? It would be the end of civilization as we know it. The next time someone tries oh-so-subtly to maneuver into your prime platform position, try using the following verbal technique:

1. "Uh," you say, "you just cut in front of me."

2. He may point out, "This isn't a line. It's more like a cluster."

3. Stand your ground: "It may not be what Webster's defines as a line, but there's some informal system in place here, and you just stepped between me and the door. That's cutting."

4. Enlist the support of those around you and appeal to their sense of justice. Make eye contact with them and ask aloud, "Am I right?" They will most likely support you, forcing the cutter to back down when he sees he's outnumbered.

ETIQUETTE TIP

In verbal confrontation, use big words and talk fast—this impresses the other person and will cause a delay in his response time as he's thinking, "Huh? What's a neophyte? Anthropomorphic? I better think of something that sounds just as smart."

Managing Anger

A subtext of the topic of etiquette is the consequences of a world without etiquette. And that's a world full of rage—road rage, elevator rage, waiting-on-line rage, in-flight rage. Anger happens. And the National Mental Health Association has these tips for dealing with it:

- Change the way you think. Replace incendiary thoughts with logical ones. For instance, turn "Oh, this is awful, everything's ruined" into "This is frustrating and it's understandable that I'm upset about it, but it's not the end of the world." Remind yourself that the world is not "out to get you"—you're just experiencing the rough spots of daily life, as everyone does.

- Learn to problem solve. But focus on coping with the problem rather than entirely solving it. You may not be able to make your train reach the station on time, but you can call the people you're meeting to let them know you'll be late and then try to get some work done during the longer-than-expected trip.

- Try to communicate better. Don't say the first thing that pops into your head. Listen to what the other person is saying and take time to think carefully before you respond.

- Use humor when appropriate. Not sarcastic, harsh humor, but constructive humor that will put your situation in perspective, such as asking the person who just cut in front of you, "Don't you know who I am? My father is the president of the United States!"

Embarking/Disembarking

Some people still haven't learned that they're supposed to let people out of the train before they begin to board. (The same goes for elevators.) The mad dash to the door causes gridlock as the people exiting meet the people entering, and the two groups bottleneck just inside the doorway. This may also lead to pandemonium as the people coming out begin to panic, thinking they're going to get carried along to the next stop. Somebody could even get trampled!

How best to educate your fellow commuters while ensuring that you have prime embarkment/disembarkment position? By leading by example, of course. The following technique works best if you're in the front of the group waiting to get on the train.

1.   When the train pulls in and the door opens, pointedly step back to let the passengers out first.

2.   If somebody sees you step back and jumps into the space in front of you—the space you have provided for disembarking passengers—explain to them: "You probably don't realize this, but people are still coming off the train. We can't get on until they're all off."

3.   Even after it looks like the last person has exited, wait a few seconds and peer inside to see if anyone else is coming. It's possible that an elderly passenger or a person loaded down with baggage is taking longer to disembark.

4.   Once the coast is clear, go ahead and get on board.

Note: In the event of bottlenecking, you're not going to be able to get on the train through this door. Immediately break left or right to the next doorway. Give a quick glance before you go to see if similar delays are hindering either side, but don't linger any longer than it takes to assess the situation.

Cell-Phone Use

It's a sign of the times that commuter trains now have Quiet Cars and provide lists of rules for proper cell-phone etiquette:

1.   Set ringers to vibrate or adjust ring level to the lowest volume.

2. Keep phone conversations to two or three minutes, maximum.

3. Keep your voice low and even.

Clearly, even the transit authority recognizes how obnoxious it is to yak loudly into your handset, and that if you do need to use a cell phone, you should use it only for emergencies—not simply to call a loved one to say, "I just got on the train," "I'm still on the train," "I'm about to get off the train."

In 1999, Japan's national communications commission issued selective licenses to live-performance theaters and concert halls to allow the use of cell-phone jamming technology. This expensive device works by preventing cell-phone reception in the specified areas. In the United States, some hospitals use these devices to prevent cell-phone signals from interfering with life-support systems. But everywhere else, citizens are left to fend for themselves. What can you do when fellow commuters remain clueless about basic courtesy? Consider the following scenario:

Fifteen minutes after boarding the train, the guy across the aisle gets a call. The ring? "Ode to Joy." He lets it play and play and play again while leisurely fishing the phone out of his pocket, and then he starts jabbering away about his day and how he almost missed the train. He goes into the whole story, laughing uproariously, gesturing at the seatback in front of him as if it's the person on the other end of the phone, oblivious to the people sitting just inches away. You would do well to give the guy the benefit of the doubt and assume he's truly unaware of the disruption he's causing.

1. Lean across the aisle and get his attention by saying, "Excuse me," loudly and firmly.

2. Wait until he makes eye contact with you.

3. Ask him to please lower his voice for the rest of the call, since there are other passengers in the car and they, like you, may be trying to read or work or think.

4. If his obnoxious behavior persists, flag down a conductor for assistance.

Of course, you might also consider taking matters in your own hands by making him the object of ridicule.

1. Once he's finished with his call, take out your own phone and call a friend whom you know won't answer.

2.   Leave a message on your friend's voicemail repeating, loudly, the story the guy just told his friend. Preface it with, "You won't believe what I just heard!"

3.   Make sure you're talking loudly enough that "Ode to Joy" Guy can hear you (but not so loudly that you would be violating the rules of cell-phone etiquette).

ON THE SUBWAY

It's fitting that the subway is underground—since people invariably turn into zombies once they enter its lair. Rude, smelly, personal-space-invading zombies, that is.

Turnstile Protocol

When a device is invented to monitor the flow of humanity—to force us to go single file like a herd of cows being rustled into their pen one by one—it's only natural that we feel resentment. Approaching a subway turnstile is knowing that you are going to have to insert a token or show a ticket and then get hit in the butt by a fast-moving metal bar for the privilege of doing so. Here are some simple tips to smooth the way:

1.   You may be tempted to jump turnstiles when no one's

around—don't. Subways are frequently monitored by closed-circuit security cameras, so your misdeed will most likely catch up with you.

2. Only one person at a time should pass through the turnstile.

3. If you are carrying a bag, hold it in front of you and above the turnstile, so it doesn't impede your passage.

4. If you are with a small child, let the child pass through first, with instructtions to wait for you on the other side.

5. If you are approaching a turnstile at exactly the same time as another rider, pause to let the other person pass before you.

6. Never attempt to hold the turnstile open for another rider. That simply defeats the purpose of the mechanism and will impede the whole system.

Pole Position

The subway-car pole is meant to assist at least four people, possibly five or six, in keeping their balance when the train pitches past curves and takes corners. Under the best of circumstances, each subway rider is aware of, and practices, proper pole-position etiquette:

1.   Position or angle your body with respect to the pole so that only one of your hands (typically your dominant hand) is in contact with the pole while the rest of your body remains approximately an arm's length away. (This allows more than one person to use the pole at any time.)

2.   Move your hand up or down the pole as needed as other passengers board and take hold of the pole.

3.   Avoid hand-to-hand contact as much as possible, maintaining your own and other's bubbles of personal space.

The pole's purpose is compromised when the rogue pole hugger boards. (Is it mere coincidence that you have only to swap the vowel in hug and it becomes hog?) The pole hog hugs the pole, whimsically swinging back and forth in half circles—sometimes completely around the pole. She's usually with a group of friends who are giddy about something—going out on the town, a movie they just saw, etc. Use the following technique to claim your rightful position:

1. Walk right up to the pole and plant your hand on it.

2. The offender may be hugging her body to the entire length of the pole. If that's the case, say, "Excuse me," to indicate that you intend to use the pole, too.

3. Once your hand is securely fastened around the pole, you'll be able to safely maneuver yourself to a comfortable standing position a few inches from it, and she'll be forced to de-hug.

How to Gross Out the Pole Hugger

This solution works best if you have a companion. If not, you'll have to make the acquaintance of someone sitting or standing near the pole hugger.

1. Find a place where you can sit or stand near the pole hugger.

2. Begin to tell your friend about a newsmagazine segment you saw—on *60 Minutes*, *Dateline*, or Yahoo!—about germs and bacteria.

3. In a voice loud enough that the pole hugger can hear, declare that researchers took samples from the poles and

handrails of a bunch of subway cars and found traces of feces.

4.   That information should clear her from the pole and make room for you—and your new companion. (Don't forget to wash your hands after disembarking.)

> **ETIQUETTE TIP**
> People don't like to be exposed to germs. If you're ever trying to get someone to vacate an area, simply drop a hint that you've got the flu, and you'll be home-free.

Seating Etiquette

The seats on the average subway car are narrow enough so that when someone's spilling into yours—well, let's just say that most fast-food-loving Americans aren't narrow enough to fit comfortably into half a seat. It's somewhat tolerable if the person in question is a bit zaftig, causing you to settle for either standing or trying to fit yourself in the remaining part of the empty seat, resting your elbows on your knees because that's the only way you'll fit. But if the rider is using a second seat for a shopping bag, a wet umbrella, or anything that could just as well fit on his lap or on the floor, you may need to take action.

The golden rule for every subway rider: No one takes up more than one seat. When you find someone who has deposited stuff on a second seat, in clear violation of the rule, try the direct approach.

1. Get the person's attention with a quick "Excuse me" and a pointed look at the shopping bag/umbrella/newspaper in the seat beside him; then turn 180 degrees and begin to lower yourself onto that seat.

2. The important thing here is not to give him a choice by asking if the seat is taken or if you can sit there. That point is moot—it's public property. You can sit there if you'd like to.

3. As you begin to sit, the person should remove the offending object from the seat. Make sure to double-check that the coast is clear before you lower all the way—the better to avoid an embarrassing incident.

The ABCs of Personal Space

History. Personal space did not become a tangible issue until the industrial revolution in the early 1800s, when people from outlying rural areas flooded into cities like London and New York.

Proxemics. The scientific name for the study of humans' behavioral use of space, pioneered in the 1960s by American anthropologist Edward T. Hall. Hall theorized that personal space is an extension of the human body, and he categorized it into four zones: the intimate zone, for whispering and embracing (within 18 inches of your body); the personal zone, for conversing with close friends (18 inches to 4 feet); the social zone, for conversing with acquaintances (4 to 10 feet); and the public zone, for interacting with strangers (10 to 25 feet).

Cultural differences. Americans require a personal zone of 6 to 8 feet, but people from Mediterranean and Asian countries, which are more densely populated, require smaller zones. In general, women sit and stand closer than men.

Deliberate space violation. Police investigators use PSIS (Personal Space Invasion Syndrome) to their advantage while interrogating a suspect—they'll deliberately stand too close to gain a psychological edge.

Pop-cultural debut. In 1994, during season five of the sitcom *Seinfeld*, the term close-talker was coined in an episode entitled "The Raincoats" to describe a character played by actor Judge Reinhold.

Giving Up Your Seat

On a crowded subway or bus, a young, healthy rider should immediately give up his or her seat for a senior citizen, a preg-

nant woman, a mother with a small child, or anyone who
seems especially in need of a seat.

1. When you see the person getting on, take the lead and
   quickly jump up from your seat.

2. Make a gesture (a sort of shoveling motion toward the
   seat combined with a questioning gaze) to the person in-
   need that indicates, "Would you like to sit?" Or, if
   they're close enough, simply ask aloud, "Would you like
   to sit?"

3. Stand in front of the seat until the passenger gets there
   to ensure that someone else doesn't take the seat first.

4. Once your passenger is safely ensconced in the seat, proceed to stand for the rest of your journey or until another seat becomes available.

Confronting the Cougher/Sneezer

When on a crowded subway—or a plane, train, or elevator
or within any enclosed space filled with other people—it's inevitable that you'll come in contact with fellow passengers'
germs. Is there anything worse than feeling another person's

microbe-ridden spray settling onto your skin? Unless your immune system is solid gold, you're almost guaranteed to come down with the offending person's cold. It's a vicious cycle—but it's a cycle that you can stop. Your actions might come too late to help yourself, but your altruism just may help countless others.

1.   Always carry tissues during flu season.

2.   Fish your tissue packet out of your bag or pocket and offer it to the sneezer or cougher.

3.   Ask, "Would you like one of these?" and smile sympathetically. "I just got over a cold myself." This will explain why you still have tissues with you and will make the offender feel like your gesture is not an affront.

4.   Should he or she refuse, just say, "Please, I insist." You may want to remind the offender of some of the basics of germ theory: "It's better that you don't give your cold to someone else."

When the helpful approach doesn't work, try the more histrionic strategy:

1. Dramatically wipe the sneezer/cougher's projectile mucus off your person. "Eeeew," you say. "Uhhh, this is gross. It's all over me!"

2. Turn to the person next to you and say, "Do you believe this? This guy gave us the weather and we didn't even want the news!"

3. The sneezer or cougher should be thoroughly embarrassed enough to cover his mouth or nose the next time.

TAXI ETIQUETTE

Depending on where you live, gaining access to a taxi can involve anything from phoning a cab company to pick you up to competing with fellow hailers on a packed street corner. Either way, chances are good that getting the cab will be just the beginning of your adventure. How can you tell whether you've flagged down an honest cabbie with an honest meter, and how should you confront him if he's not? What are the guidelines for tipping? What about sharing the ride? And what happens when your driver tries to get a little too friendly?

Competitive Hailing

Native New Yorkers track taxis like hunters stalk deer. Standing on a corner, blending into their natural habitat, eyes scanning the streets, mouths twitching with impatience, they have an uncanny knack for spotting the rectangular light box that, when lit, means "vacant and on duty"—even when it's four blocks away. You may have been standing on that corner longer, but how can you compete with a lifelong cab wrangler? It's in their blood. What should you do when they hail the taxi that should've been yours?

The most effective approach is to meet the hailer's expertise with some city smarts of your own.

1. Edging toward where the hailer is standing, ask where she's headed.

2. If you're going in the same direction, ask if she wants to share the cab.

3. If she's not willing to share, take advantage of her momentary hesitation and jump in the backseat, yelling your destination to the driver so he can peel away from the curb and leave your competitor in the dust.

4. Stop feeling guilty—you were there first.

Alternatively (and especially if you're weighed down with bags on both arms), you may simply want to evoke the expert hailer's pity.

1. Exclaim what a great hailer of taxis she is. "I can't believe it! You had your hand up when that cab was still four blocks away."

2. Then despair over your own taxi-hailing skills. "I'm just so bad at getting cabs. You'd think I'd see them sooner since they're bright yellow and lit up at night, but I'm just not a city person." Giggle. (This is called playing dumb.)

3. Go in for the kill. "Would you mind if I took this cab? It'll take me so long to find another one, and it'll only take you a second."

Even jaded city folk will be flattered and/or moved by your appeal and graciously step aside. If they don't, refer back to the initial approach (see step 3).

Cabbie Relations

Okay, so you've got your cab—now you need to move into phase two: forming a favorable relationship with your cab driver. Ideally it's one based on honesty and good faith, but since the cabbie may not always be so virtuous, you must enter into it clear-eyed, and with a healthy amount of wariness.

Meter Reading

The first rule of thumb for any self-respecting taxi passenger is this: Keep an eagle eye on that meter. Chances are you've ridden cabs in this city before, so you know how much you're supposed to be charged per mile and when extra charges come into play. If it looks like the fare is not adding up, speak up.

1.   Express concern: "Hmm, that's strange. I've ridden this route before and the fare was never this high. Have fares gone up and I just haven't heard about it?"

2.   This mild form of confrontation may prompt your driver to fess up in a roundabout way, admitting that his meter is "broken." Travel authorities advise anyone riding in a cab with a broken meter to immediately get out and notify the cab company. It's against the law for a driver to even be out on the road with a broken meter, and he or she is subject to a fine.

3.   Or, if you'd rather avoid confrontation with a large, angry cabbie, jot down his name, registration number, and the cab company's phone number, and call the com-

pany once you're safely home to demand reimbursement. Of course, if you choose to pay the bogus fare, you're under no obligation to tip.

4.   If, when you get in the cab, the meter isn't working at all and the driver wants to negotiate a flat fee with you, it's your call. If you're familiar with the route, know how much it costs, and can settle on a fare that seems right, that's one thing. If you're new to the city and vulnerable to a dishonest driver—a broken meter is already a sign that he's not on the up and up—you are within your rights to get out and take the next cab.

A Tipping Exercise

Connect the scenario with the tip it deserves (listed as percentages of the total fare). Note: Experts estimate that the correct tip for a taxi driver is 15 percent of the fare, with a $1 minimum.

1.   The cabbie turns a 10-minute trip into a 20-minute escapade and doesn't follow the route you've requested.

2.   The cab stops short so many times, you're getting whiplash.

3.   The cabbie gets you to your destination in time, but you've

had to endure hearing him yak away about his marriage trouble.

4.   The cabbie gets you to your destination and, having determined you're a tourist, gives you some history about the area.

    a. 15 percent
    b. 20 percent
    c. 0 percent

Answers: 1. c (it's a rider's right to determine the route); 2. a (yes, a miserable ride, but he got you to your destination, so he gets the bare minimum); 3. a (see 2. a); 4. b (an extra effort deserves an extra-fat tip).

The Overly Friendly Cabbie

Well, it's better than the mean-spirited cabbie—you know, the guy who's having a really bad day and takes it out on you? When Rudy Giuliani was mayor of New York, he required that all taxi drivers take a four-hour course on courtesy and customer service. He was responding to one particularly embarrassing year when the city's taxi and limousine commission received more than 4,600 rudeness complaints. Among the tips handed down to cabbies taking the course: "Exchange pleasantries; show your passenger you're happy he's in your cab; treat your passenger like a guest."

Sometimes, however, such niceties can go too far, and your driver won't stop exchanging anecdotes and small talk and bad jokes and, well, you get the idea. Driving a cab can be lonely, yes. But as a passenger, you have the right to a conversation-free ride.

1.   As with "Defending against the Garrulous Seatmate" in the "In Flight" section (see page 21), your first defense is, Show, don't tell. Pull out some reading material or work from your bag or briefcase. With head down (so that no eye contact can be made via the rearview mirror), act as if you're absorbed in whatever you're reading. Start jotting down notes.

2.   If you have a cell phone, pull it out and make a call (you can fake it if you really don't want to call anyone). He can't talk while you're talking to someone else.

3.   Finally, if he's still not understanding these subtle hints, ask him point-blank: "Do you mind if we don't talk during this ride?"

ON THE HIGHWAYS AND BYWAYS

A recent study of driving behavior by a Michigan firm revealed that 80 percent of people are angry while they're driving. And, really, is that surprising? The bulk of these people are working office or factory jobs, toiling away to make another person some money, their every minute accounted for even if they're just going outside for air or to smoke. Finally, they get on the road and then they're in charge. The king or queen of their vehicle. When someone has the audacity to tailgate or flash high beams at them—the king, the master of the road—watch out, here comes trouble.

It doesn't have to be this way. There are proper ways to behave in traffic, even under the most stressful conditions. And if enough people simply obeyed the golden rule of the road (Do Unto Other Drivers as You Would Have Them Do Unto You), our highways and byways would be much kinder and gentler places. This golden rule encompasses a series of technical rules taught in driver's education class—such as when to use high beams and low beams and signals—that should be second nature. Unfortunately, some people never took the time to learn them or choose to disregard them.

(Note: Contrary to common perceptions, Americans are not the only drivers who repress their anger all day and then take it out on the road; the term road rage was in fact coined in England. And, yes, researchers have even uncovered instances of "buggy rage" in colonial times.)

Here are some of the basic driving rules—just in case you've forgotten your driver's ed. Violating any one of these may make you the target of road rage.

- Lane blocking. The left lane is the passing lane—use it only for that purpose. Stay out of the left lane and yield to the right for any vehicle that wants to overtake you.

- Tailgating. Don't do it. Maintain a safe distance between your car and the car in front of you.

- Signal use. Drivers may accuse you of cutting them off if you don't signal before switching lanes. Give them ample notice by switching on your turn signal. Make sure to turn it off once you've successfully changed lanes or turned.

- Horn use. Use the horn only when absolutely necessary, and, when you do, tap it lightly. Refrain from impatient behavior, like honking at the person in front of you as soon as the light turns green—the jarring noise could set off a stressed-out motorist.

- Merging. Move out of the right-hand lane to allow vehicles entering from ramps to merge easily.

- Blocking traffic. If you see a friend walking on the sidewalk and you want to converse with him, do not block traffic to do so. Pull over to the side of the road (or just pretend you never saw the friend and keep going).

- Electronic devices. Don't fuss with your phone while you're driving—dialing, texting, and the like. Taking your mind off the road isn't just rude, it's dangerous. And it's illegal in many places, besides. That goes for your GPS, too. Do your navigational programming while your vehicle is safely in park, not while you're driving.

Beamers

Have you ever been driving along a dark country road late at night with your high beams on? You see another car approaching, so you turn your beams to low to avoid momentarily blinding the other driver. The other driver, however, forgets to turn her beams to low.

1.   Blink your lights—from high to low and back—to indi-
      cate to the other driver that something is amiss.

2.   If she ignores your signaling and keeps her high beams
      lit, use your hand to shield your eyes and avoid being
      blinded by the bright light. To stay your course, focus
      your gaze on the white or yellow stripe that separates
      your two lanes.

3.   Alternatively, if a driver is inching up behind you with
      high beams on and the light is bouncing off your
      rearview mirror and into your face, slow down to let
      him pass.

Cooperative Highway Driving

While driving on the highway, you may encounter some poor
soul who realizes, just as he's about to pass the turnoff ramp,
that he's about to miss his exit. Unfortunately, he's two lanes
away and will try, frantically, to maneuver quickly over those
two lanes. You'll probably see him gesticulating and pointing
toward the exit to indicate that that's where he's trying to go.

1.   Help him out, but first make sure you can do so safely;
      look in your rearview mirror to see if there's anyone

close behind you.

2.   If there's no one close behind, slow down and wave him into your lane.

3.   Once he passes through your lane and onto the exit ramp, resume your previous cruising speed.

Identifying the Road Warrior

There is no one portrait of the aggressive driver. Ragers can be young or old; male or female (although the majority of cases involve male aggressors); Hispanic, black, Asian, or white. According to the AAA Foundation for Traffic Safety, "There are hundreds of aggressors who are successful men and women . . . with no known histories of crime, violence, or alcohol and drug abuse." Even actor Jack Nicholson—an Oscar winner!—believing another car had cut him off, once stepped out of his car at a red light and went at the other car's windshield and roof with a golf club. (See page 53 for the most common road-rage weapons.)

All of which makes it nearly impossible to positively identify a road rager in advance—though you can look for typical stress triggers. For example, is the driver dealing with a car full of unruly children? Is the person in a suit, indicating that he's in a frustrating corporate job, maybe even middle management? Look at the person's facial expression—is his or her jaw clenched or brows knit together? Can he or she be seen mouthing obscenities or making obscene gestures? If so, avoid making eye contact and follow the rules of the road.

Anatomy of Road Rage

According to a study by the Automobile Association Group Public Policy Road Safety Unit, road rage most commonly manifests itself in the following forms:

- Aggressive tailgating
- Repeated headlight flashing
- Obscene gestures
- Deliberately obstructing other vehicles
- Verbal abuse

Weapons Used by Aggressive Drivers

Road rage at its most intense level involves violence. If you come into contact with a road rager, here's what you can expect to be used to injure you or damage your vehicle:

1. Feet and fists.
2. Tire irons and jack handles.

3.   Baseball bats.
4.   Knives, including bayonets, ice picks, razor blades, and swords.
5.   Projectiles such as beer bottles and partially eaten foods.
6.   Golf clubs, lead pipes, crowbars, canes, and hatchets.
7.   Defensive sprays.

Since most instances of road rage stem from high stress levels, consider taking the following measures to avoid letting yourself become uncontrollably enraged:

1.   Alter your schedule to avoid the worst traffic congestion, even if it means leaving for work a little early or staying at your desk an hour longer to avoid rush-hour traffic.

2.   Improve the comfort of your car. Make sure your air-conditioning and heating systems work effectively. Stock up on CDs or MP3 playlists of relaxing music. Make sure your windshield is clean and clear.

3.   Avoid anger-inducing talk radio.

4.   Learn relaxation techniques to use when in a stressful situation, such as traffic gridlock. These include breath-

ing deeply, loosening your grip on the wheel, doing limited stretches for your arms and legs, and becoming aware that your jaw is clenched and consciously unclenching it.

5.   Avoid driving when you know you're in a bad mood.

6.   Prepare for your trip—know how to get where you're going, approximate how much time it will take, and bring a map and a cell phone in case you need to call for directions.

ETIQUETTE TIP

When faced with a raging motorist, we suggest that you refrain from using the one-fingered salute. Though a little rage is healthy, this gesture sometimes provokes violent behavior in the other party, which is not to your advantage. Restraint should be the order of the day.

Retaliation

Sometimes, however, restraint is not nearly as sweet as revenge. You, too, can allow yourself to revel in your own road rage, as long as you're not breaking any laws in the process. So they don't like it when you're going the speed limit, eh?

They're ready to risk your life and the lives of others by cutting into the next lane and then cutting in front of you? You can play that game.

1.   Maneuver out of your lane, speed up, and pull into the lane in front of the offending driver.

2.   Once you're in position, slow down so you're traveling just at the speed limit.

3.   When the driver show signs of becoming enraged—honking, yelling, becoming red faced (you can check in your rearview mirror)—maintain your maddeningly steady speed. Ah, that feels good.

Incendiary Bumper Stickers

You have every right to flaunt the particular nuances of your obnoxious worldview. Just be prepared for the consequences if you display stickers on your car that are meant to incite, such as a Confederate flag, a prochoice or prolife sentiment, or statements such as "I like my women barefoot and pregnant," all of which you may think are funny but could just possibly be misconstrued as offensive.

Competitive Parking

If you own a car and you live in an area more populous than, say, East Nowhere, you'll need a good grasp of basic parking skills. And even if you're in East Nowhere, chances are you have to drive to the nearest strip mall just like the residents of the five other towns nearby—which means you may have to fight for your right to that parking space. Following the basic rules of parking etiquette can help head off any nasty confrontations.

1. Always signal your intentions when pulling into a parking space from moving traffic. You can either go "head in" or "tail in" when parallel parking, but you'll find that most state driving manuals recommend the tail-in maneuver.

2. Choose a designated parking space that you are sure is long and/or wide enough for your vehicle. Make certain that the cars around you have seen you and are prepared to move around you, and that there's enough room for them to do so. Do not create a traffic hazard.

3. When parallel parking, look behind you both ways to make sure your path is clear of pedestrians.

4. When parallel parking, do not tap the vehicles in front

of or behind you. This is not what bumpers are for.

5.   Never take up more than one parking space. If the parking spaces are not demarcated, simply pull up within 12 inches of the car in front of you or on either side of you. In a parallel parking situation, the space must allow enough room for the persons in front of you and behind you to get out of their spaces. In a parking lot, make sure there's enough room on either side so that your car door does not hit another vehicle when you're exiting or entering your car.

6.   Never park in a handicapped parking spot unless you're legally entitled to do so.

But what to do when another driver hasn't followed the rules, leading you to become rightfully enraged? Say you're in the mall parking lot, driving through the aisles, looking for an empty space. You see someone's rear lights go on, indicating they're about to reverse out of the spot. You stop and put on your turn signal. From the other side of the aisle comes another car, an SUV, whose driver has the audacity to turn on *his* turn signal. But you were there first!

Uh-uh. No way. That space is yours. It belongs to you. You're going to park, and then you're going to shop—it's your

God-given right.

1.   Assuming that the other driver is simply clueless and not homicidal (see page 59 for how to ID road warrior), try to make eye contact. The person in the other car may be a couple of feet higher than you are (like they really need that all-terrain vehicle).

2.   Once contact has been made, begin to gesticulate. Point to the space, or to the car pulling out of the space, and then point to yourself as if to say, "That space? It's mine." Nod your head all the while: "Yup, mine."

3.   Inch up a little closer, still leaving room for the retreating car to back out but just enough to let the other car know you're going to stand your ground.

4.   If the other car is still there, resume the gesticulating. Shake your head as if to say, "I'm not budging." Point to the space again and then wave the other car away.

CHAPTER 2

AT THE OFFICE

It's a sad state of affairs when the thought of spending another day at work is enough to make you contemplate throwing yourself in front of an oncoming subway car. It's not just the boring drudgery or the confounding office politics—it's the little things, like the fact that you're boxed into a cubicle whose walls are so thin, you can hear your neighbor's chipper phone greeting over and over . . . and over again, even after you're home and in bed. It's the photocopier that's always jammed, the printer that always needs its toner replaced, and the communal kitchen that always smells like milk gone bad. If everyone paid more attention to these supposed trivialities, work would be a better place, and we could all deal much better with those canceled holiday bonuses and pay/promotion freezes.

Photocopier Etiquette

Here's what to expect from an office machine: that it functions consistently at its highest level. And though machines may malfunction because of old age or missing parts, usually when an office machine isn't working, it's because of human error. We must remember that the photocopier is a delicate mechanism that, when properly fed and cared for, will provide the average worker with limitless productivity and hundreds of pristine copies—collated and stapled, no less—every workday.

But the photocopier is only as efficient as the people who use it, and in a busy office that means coworkers must cooperate when it comes to making sure the machine is well tended at all times. Following the essentials of copier etiquette is the best way to start.

1.   Never leave the copier without first attending to a flashing icon, which usually indicates a paper jam or misfeed or the need for a new toner cartridge.

2.   If you cannot resolve the copier's distress signal by yourself, notify your office manager or machine serviceperson immediately.

3.   Never leave the copy machine empty of paper.

4. If you used colored paper or letterhead or any type of paper besides white, remove it before leaving the machine so that others don't use it by mistake.

5. If you become frustrated with the copy machine, do not kick it, punch it, or become violent toward it in any way.

6. Do not eat or drink around the photocopier.

7. Do not smudge the platen glass with your oily fingertips.

8. No matter how funny it looked in the movie, do not attempt to photocopy your own or another's body parts.

9. Remove staples, sticky notes, and paper clips from whatever you're going to copy.

10. Little jobs trump big jobs. If you're making five copies of a 250-page report, you should interrupt the job to let in the person who needs to make a one-page copy.

Copier Courtesy in Action

Your boss has given you another annoying copying task—to categorize all of her receipts from a recent business trip to Europe into Food, Entertainment, and Transportation, then to copy them all onto separate pieces of paper, in triplicate, for her expense report.

There are about 37 receipts, and you're already at the copier, arranging the little bits of paper on the platen glass, when a coworker approaches.

Gingerly he steps up, holding a single piece of paper. Letting him cut in front of you would mean having to rearrange all of these receipts. What do you do?

1. Ask him how many copies he needs to make.

2. If it's under 10, gallantly interrupt your job to let him make his copies.

3. Remove all your papers from the copier and step aside, gesturing to the copier and insisting, "You go ahead. I'm going to be here forever."

4. Once he makes his copies and thanks you for letting him cut in, proceed with your own job.

Of course, some surly coworkers derive sadistic pleasure from making people with small jobs wait . . . and wait . . . and wait. How to handle this situation?

1.   Confront him. Say, "Excuse me. Do you mind if I cut in and just make these four copies?"

2.   If he says no, insisting either that his flow cannot be interrupted or that he was there first, ask him how much longer he'll be.

3.   If he has no sense of protocol, appeal to his logic. Point out all of the copies he still has to make and the very few that you need to make.

4.   Point out that your meeting starts in five minutes—and he just said he'd be there past five minutes.

5.   If he still doesn't budge, make a mental note of this unpleasant episode. Resolve to practice a little harmless "voodoo" (see page 77) on him as soon as you return to your desk.

Outing the Office Saboteur

Who are those office saboteurs who leave the fax machine paperless after using the last sheet or who abandon the photocopier once they've jammed it? Unless the writing on the paper that you extract from Areas A through D provides a clue, it's impossible to know. You may need to undertake some office surveillance to catch the culprit in the act, enlisting the help of those whose offices or cubicles are close to the machine. Once you find out who it is, let everyone else know so that the person responsible is thereafter shunned from happy hours and sneered at in the hallways.

A time-honored and less time-consuming approach is to post an admonishing sign near the copier. This is more a gesture than an effective solution—it doesn't really spur anyone into action—but it is useful as a venting device:

1. Design the sign on your computer—it will look more official and be taken more seriously than if it is written by hand.

2. Make it slightly funny. Acknowledge that it's extremely annoying when the paper jams or when the fax runs out of paper, but ask that whoever is present when such an event occurs please remedy the situation. Possible wording: "To all: Yes, you're having a bad day and the last thing you want to do is fix that pesky paper jam or refill the paper you just used up. Just do it!"

3. Sign it "The Management" to instill some fear that Big Brother is indeed watching.

4.   Print it out and post it prominently over the copier.

The Communal Kitchen

Out wafts the stink of old cheese and meat from the refrigerator; the sink is filled with soiled coffee mugs and dishes; the countertop is a mess of old stains and crumbs. These are all signs that your officemates are total pigs. But it doesn't have to be this way. The best way to ensure that the communal kitchen is less of a haven for mice and roaches is to set a good example. (And if that fails, take it up with the management. No manager likes the prospect of a hantavirus outbreak in the office.)

1.   If you made the mess, clean it up.

2.   Don't just leave your plastic lunch containers to soak in the sink—chances are you'll forget them. Wash them right away.

3.   If you prepare food on the counter, wipe it off when you're finished.

4.   Never leave anything in the refrigerator longer than a week.

5.   If you take the last cup of coffee, turn off the coffeepot and rinse it out; if you take the last doughnut, throw away the box.

6.   If you have many department meetings or mini office parties where food is served, set up an alternating system where clean-up duties are equally dispersed.

7.   Don't take anyone else's food or beverage from the fridge or cabinets without asking first.

8.   Store only edible items in the communal kitchen, not science experiments or your pet's stool samples.

Dealing with the Overripe Communal Refrigerator

Perhaps the most selfless task an office worker can perform for his coworkers is to take on the cleaning of a nasty communal refrigerator. Perhaps you're motivated by guilt, since you know that several of the shoddily wrapped sources of stink are your own; maybe you're a saint. Either way, here's how it's done.

1.   Wear rubber gloves and some kind of face mask so as not to pass out when you open the door.

2.   Gather your cleaning products nearby—bleach, disinfectant, and plenty of sponges.

3.   Put on your gloves and face gear and begin by removing everything from the refrigerator and placing it in a nearby trashcan. Even those items that are not yet rancid have been contaminated by their proximity to the overripe foodstuffs.

4.   Once the shelves are empty, spray ample amounts of disinfectant over the entire surface and wipe it clean with a sponge.

5.   Repeat step 4 several times to completely eradicate the lingering odor.

6.   Now apply a layer of bleach to thoroughly disinfect the interior.

7.   Wipe clean with a wet sponge.

The Office Gift

Once the first e-mail comes around asking everyone to chip in for a coworker's birthday present, birthday cake, baby shower, good-bye present, and so forth, it creates a domino effect, and the occasions to chip in just keep coming. And then the chipping in begins to chip away at your net salary—a dollar here, five bucks there—so that you begin to think twice the next time you get a "chip-in" e-mail. How well do you really know or like the person anyway? Would you get this person a present on your own if the occasion called for it? Probably not. (How many people at work do you actually *like*?)

The parameters for office gift giving are as follows:

1. All requests for chip-ins should come with a suggested contribution range (from $1 to $10) and the caveat that participating is optional.

2. The collector of the chip-ins should not make the rounds, entering people's workspaces to ask for their contribution; those who want to chip in should do so of their own volition. No one should be subjected to pressure tactics.

3. The collector should never reveal how much was given by each person.

4. If you work in the gift recipient's department, a contribution is called for.

5.   If you're a low-level employee, you should not be expected to give at the high end of the range.

6.   Contributions to gifts for people outside your department should be made on a case-by-case basis, reflecting the closeness of your working relationship.

7.   Interns are exempt from giving.

8.   Everyone, regardless of whether they've chipped in or not, should be welcome to attend the accompanying office party.

Should you choose not to contribute to the group gift, simply opt out. If the person collecting money asks why you do not wish to contribute, just shrug and say something vague, like you're a little short this month. There's no need to explain your position. The e-mail requesting contributions should have included an optional clause (see rule no. 1) so that people who choose not to participate can do so without guilt.

Kibitzing with Coworkers

Hopefully you're in a job where you like and respect your coworkers—you have fun joking around at meetings and sharing your observations about the day's headlines or the previous night's TV shows.

Still, the line between casual kibitzing and coworker harassment is a fine one, and there are rules about not crossing it. It's important to be able to read the signs that indicate when it's time to stop chatting and let your coworker get back to work.

It's OK to kibitz:

1.   When your coworker looks genuinely interested in what you have to say.

2.   When you have a few minutes on your hands before a meeting and you stay no longer than that.

3.   When your coworker calls you in to talk.

4.   When your coworker is sharing his own experiences and asking you questions about yours.

5.   When it's a Friday afternoon during the summer. (Nothing's getting done, anyway.)

Top 6 clues indicating that it's not time to kibitz:

1.   Your coworker's body language is sending a clear message (averted gaze, turning back to computer monitor,

looking in drawers).

2.   The guest chair in your coworker's office is piled high with paper, and he makes no attempt to clear it when you enter the room.

3.   Your coworker is eating.

4.   Your coworker looks harried.

5.   Your coworker's door is closed.

6.   Your coworker's head is down on his desk.

Dealing with the Kibitzer Who Won't Quit

"So, what's new?" "Did you hear?" "How are you?" It doesn't matter how it starts—you know how it's going to end. This coworker, the one with a nickname for everyone in the office, will continue to stand in your doorway talking about nothing you care to know—office gossip, his weekend—while you continue to hint that you have a lot of work to do. You have two options:

Option A. Leave your office.

1. Get up and leave your office to get coffee or water or to use the restroom. He may walk you to your destination, perhaps even continue to talk while you go to the bathroom, or decide that he, too, needs some coffee.

2. When you get back to your office, stop outside for a second and say, "Well, Tom, I'll see you later," then close your door behind you. If you don't have a door, give him an extra look of finality, sit down at your desk, pick up your phone, and start dialing a number.

Option B. Receive an urgent e-mail.

1. Check your e-mail inbox as he's talking.

2. Pretend that one of the e-mails you've just opened is urgent and needs your immediate attention. (Assume an oh-my-gosh look.)

3. The nosy parker will immediately want to know what's up. Promise him you'll tell him later and then say, "I have to deal with this right away. Would you mind closing the door?"

4.   Pick up the phone and start dialing numbers.

Cubicle Courtesy

A study completed in 2001 by an environmental psychologist at Cornell University confirms what we all already know: Cubicles are not fit for humans. The scientist studied 40 women working in cubicles where the atmosphere ranged from very quiet to one suffused with typical office background noise. The women in the noisier cubicles experienced much higher stress levels, made 40 percent fewer attempts to solve an unsolvable puzzle, and were more prone to twisting themselves into nonergonomic positions (which left them open to repetitive stress injuries). And it's not just the noise that makes cubicles lousy places to work—it's the size. Where cubicles once averaged an area of eight feet by eight feet, they're now closer to five feet by six feet, providing 30 square feet of workspace—or half as much space as the average jail cell.

To make these doorless, anonymous spaces livable for you and your coworkers, be sure to keep in mind the basics of cubicle courtesy.

1.   When on the phone, keep your voice low and even.

2.   Avoid noisemakers: Set cell phones and pagers to vi-

brate; turn off the sound on your computer; if you're going on vacation, turn the ringer on your phone to the "off" position; wear headphones if you like to listen to music or the radio while you work.

3. Refrain from backing your chair into the cubes' "common wall."

4. Keep personal phone calls especially hush-hush (no one wants to know what you did last night, and if they do want to know—you don't want them to know) and to no longer than five minutes. Even better, make the call during lunch or after work, or use e-mail.

5. Respect the space of others. Just because they don't have a door doesn't mean you should feel free to barge in at will. Knock or pause to make sure they're not busy before you enter.

6. Don't stand around and wait to speak to a coworker who's on the phone or speaking to another coworker. Come back in a few minutes.

7. Avoid bringing strong smells into close working quarters—avoid too much perfume or cologne—and always

remember to use deodorant. Do not eat strong-smelling foods at your desk, such as cheesy microwave popcorn or anything with raw onions.

Dealing with the Cubicle Neighbor You'd Like to Kill

After just two months on the job, you've become intimately familiar with your next-door neighbor's quirks. All that separates you is a flimsy wall that's made of fabric that's only a quarter-inch thick. So by now you know that your neighbor tends to assume a Southern accent whenever she's talking to someone down South, that she uses the same tired jokes over and over—"What did the Dalai Lama say to the hot dog vendor? Make me one with everything"—and that she hums the Muppet Show theme song while she's working. She's programmed her computer to say "Oopsie" when she makes a mistake. Even the way she answers her phone, with a slight lilt to her name, is becoming unbearably annoying.

Option A. Ask Her to Be Quiet; Wear Ear Buds; Create White Noise.

You have every right to ask her to cut out the humming. Just ask politely. If you're on relatively good terms—and she's not deliberately trying to annoy you—she'll try to stop. Maybe she's one of those for whom humming is a reflex, in which case, just remind her with a, "Liz? Do you mind . . . ?"

As for the things you can't really ask her not to do—for example, "Can you please stop being an infuriatingly annoying human being?"—you'll need a different approach. Bring headphones to work to listen to music or a small radio that you can play quietly to create some noise other than whatever's coming from her mouth. Use a midfrequency sound machine, one that creates white noise to drown out her constant chatter.

Option B. Voodoo

When the situation gets out of hand—when you can't stand it any longer—the best thing to do is seek a (relatively) healthy outlet for your anger. Create a voodoo doll of your cubicle neighbor.

1. Form a cross with two twigs or ice-pop sticks, tying them together with twine or string.

2. Glue cotton stuffing to the twigs or sticks.

3. Acquire a piece of fabric (any type) that's big enough to lay over the doll in a diamond shape.

4. Wrap the fabric around the doll with one hand while tying it in place with ribbon or string with your other hand. To make it look more bodylike, tie the string in an X shape.

5. Embellish the doll with decorations: Inscribe your cubicle mate's name on the fabric; attach some physical object from her cubicle that won't be missed and that carries her vibration; if possible, attach a photograph.

6. Draw symbols on the doll: a gaping mouth through which she talks and talks and talks; a thundercloud to symbolize the misfortune that will befall her.

7. As you stick the doll with pins, cast your hexes aloud. For example: "You will get in a rut / and receive a big fat paper cut," or "The copier hates you, too / which is why it will jam on you."

8. Don't let anyone at work know you are doing this.

Office E-mail

Too bad the Internet didn't come with a guidebook, or at the very least some elementary e-mail dos and don'ts (see page

206 for tips on recreational e-mail). Though in some ways e-mail has made our lives easier—by cutting down reply time and allowing a less confrontational option than face-to-face communication—it also has a frightening tendency to take over our lives. The average office worker receives 50 e-mails each day, and about 40 percent of the commercial e-mails in your inbox are spam. Think of all the time spent deleting spam and replying to the rest. Then there's basic Netiquette to take into consideration, correct and incorrect ways to compose and reply to interoffice e-mails, as well as rules for when it's proper to forward a crude joke, when not to hit "Reply All" (hint: when you're about to get personal), and not spamming your coworkers.

When composing interoffice e-mail, keep the basic rules in mind.

1. Include a greeting line, with or without "Dear" as a modifier, depending on your relationship with the person you're communicating with. If you're not on a first-name basis with the recipient, you need to use the proper title (Mr., Mrs., Ms.) as well as his or her first and last name.

2. Proper use of punctuation, grammar, and capitalization is not optional.

3. Do not overuse exclamation points. Though it may be difficult to communicate your tone in an e-mail, this tactic is the in-person equivalent of giggling too often at inappropriate times.

4. Do not use emoticons in interoffice e-mails.

5. Give your e-mail a relevant, specific subject line so that the recipient will be able to find it easily weeks or months later.

6. Keep your signature line professional: Include your title and contact information, but lose the inspirational quote and/or insipid "Have a great day!"

7. Do not spam your fellow coworkers by sending out general messages to the entire office.

8. Remember that e-mails are easily forwarded to other parties, unbeknownst to you, so do not include personal information that you don't want others to see.

When a Correspondent's Sig Line Has Run Its Course

When you simply can't contain yourself from commenting on a correspondent's stale sig line, remember to use a dose of humor so she's not completely offended:

- Say something like, "I'd like to file a complaint—I'm no longer inspired by your quote."

- Directly reference the quote in a postscript: "By the way, I feel that I've changed my life sufficiently to capitalize on making the best of every minute of every day—now tell me what to do next."

Once she's gently reminded to change the saying, you'll have the chance to be freshly annoyed by the next one.

ETIQUETTE TIP

When confronted with a particularly obnoxious sig line, try countering it with a nonmotivational one of your own: Go through quote books, transcripts of George Carlin shows, or whatever it takes to find that perfect gem—a truly pessimistic remark that says, basically, life sucks.

Forwarding E-mail

Stupid jokes about what makes men different from women, lists of how you know you grew up in the 1980s, religious messages, quizzes to calculate how well you know your friend, motivational anecdotes—so much crap is generated in the world, and most of it seems to end up in your e-mail inbox. In a professional workplace, it's important to think twice before forwarding, following these guidelines:

1. Do not forward indiscriminately to everyone in your address book just because you think an e-mail is funny. Take into account your contact's sense of humor. If, after five minutes, you still think he'll find it funny, send it, but apologize in advance.

2. Part of being selective about what you choose to forward is filtering out the real trash: refrain from forwarding goofy doctored images, clearly bogus petitions that will make the world a better place, chain letters, pleas to save public television, fabricated "missing little girl" e-mails, and so forth. Think twice before sending quizzes, petitions, and pleas for money.

3. Don't forward huge graphic attachments that might either crash a friend's computer or take forever to open.

4. Do not forward e-mail meant only for you.

5. Do not forward religious messages to your agnostic and

atheist friends—proselytizing via e-mail is just as annoying as it is in person.

6.   Do not forward anything that someone might find offensive (e.g., sending a pictures of a kitten trapped in a jar to a cat lover).

Flaming

Without the verbal cues and gestures that are the hallmarks of face-to-face communication, it's easy to misinterpret the tone or intent of a coworker's e-mail. In situations when you are unsure how to interpret a message, ask your correspondent directly, in person, to clarify any misunderstandings. Assume the best intentions, and do not be confrontational. At all costs, do not let your e-mail replies degenerate to the level of "flaming" (and make sure your own messages do not resort to incendiary language).

1.   Take deep breaths and count to 10 before replying to any e-mails that "push your buttons."

2.   If you're sure your correspondent is trying to provoke you, consider simply ignoring the flame.

3.   If you must reply, take the high road, refraining from

devolving into cheap shots and unprofessional language. Make sure your points are well founded, and back them up within the e-mail.

4.   If your correspondent continues to flame, suggest a face-to-face meeting where you can come to terms with the issue under discussion.

Answering E-mails

Treat an office e-mail just as you would a phone call or letter; the courtesy of a reply is expected and required, even if it's just a few short lines acknowledging receipt.

1.   Reply to the e-mail promptly, even if it's only to say that you won't be able to provide a more satisfying response for a day or two because you're swamped with a project.

2.   If it's been weeks or days since your correspondent wrote, begin your reply with an apology for not writing back sooner, and offer some explanation.

3.   When replying, make sure you're replying to the right person, so that sensitive material does not end up in the wrong hands. (Be careful not to hit "Reply All" if you don't mean to).

Office Phone Etiquette

The phone is one step up on the interpersonal communication scale from e-mail—that is, it's more directly interactive and requires more attentiveness (there's no time to ponder your responses and catch yourself before you respond inappropriately). In the workplace, phone calls should be direct, to the point, and restricted to the professional plane.

1.   When answering the phone, identify yourself by stating your name.

2.   When placing a call, identify yourself and give the name of your company.

3.   Keep conversations focused and direct; do not assume the person on the other end has unlimited time to chat with you. Keep the small talk to a minimum.

4.   Be selective about phone use. If the purpose of your communication can be more efficiently communicated via e-mail, then compose and send a message instead.

5.   When leaving a voicemail message, remember to speak slowly and distinctly and to give your name, phone number, and date and time of your call.

6.   Reply to all voicemail or other phone messages in a timely manner, allowing no more than a day to pass.

7.   Do not use speakerphone unless it's absolutely necessary—for example, when there's more than one person in the room who needs to be part of the conversation. Always notify the person on the other end that you're about to put them on speakerphone.

8.   When you're going on vacation, remember to change your voicemail message, indicating the days you'll be out of the office, so callers will know why you're not returning their calls.

The Office Bathroom

The office bathroom is a place that calls for high attention to civility. Sharing a jail-cell-sized space with a fellow cubicle inhabitant violates our personal-space boundaries, but performing our most private bodily functions in the proximity of mere acquaintances does so even more. When navigating this uncharted territory, keep in mind the following:

1.   Except in instances of dire emergency, never monopolize the bathroom for more than 10 minutes. (Do your

magazine reading elsewhere.)

2.   Always choose the stall farthest from any already occu-
      pied stalls.

3.   Replace the toilet-paper roll when only a few squares
      remain.

4.   Do not begin or continue a conversation with a coworker
      once she has entered and locked a stall.

5.   Refrain from posting obscenities or limericks featuring
      your coworkers or boss on bathroom walls.

6.   Refrain from taking communal reading material into the
      stall with you.

7.   Wash your hands with soap before returning to work.

Office-Speak

Despite the rise of e-mail, face-to-face interaction—whether
during meetings or one-on-one—is still the standard mode of
communication at most companies. But verbal interactions
can become frustrating when colleagues are purposefully

vague or patronizing, or when they latch on to buzzwords to show that they're "team players" and to signal how ingrained they are in the culture. (These are the employees who will compare everything to something sports related.) When communicating or presenting at meetings or other work venues, keep these rules in mind:

1.   Use terms that everyone can easily comprehend. If you're presenting a report on a little-known aspect of the business at a meeting, for instance, begin with a brief explanation in straightforward layperson's terms.

2.   Unless you work for a sports network, refrain from using baseball, basketball, and any other sports analogies.

3.   Keep annoying coinages out of your speech: no talk of "synergy," "growing" the company, or "marrying" concepts.

4.   Avoid euphemisms. If it's been a bad year, say so. Don't use "reorganization" when you mean staff cuts; don't use "thinking outside the box" when you mean creativity.

5.   Refrain from using "street" language to indicate how with it you are.

CHAPTER 3

BIG-CITY LIVING

With all these people living closely together, it's inevitable that you will either witness or be a victim of a crime; you'll need to negotiate bustling street corners and deal with the dreaded "slow walkers"; you'll get buzzed by a rollerblader or a biker; you'll encounter noisy dogs and noisy neighbors—and that's just for starters.

With all these realities of urban life, you need to know the basic rules of civil behavior that make life in the big city much easier to bear.

ON THE STREETS

City streets are witness to any number of etiquette violations and general bad behavior. When venturing forward in the city, you must be prepared to encounter the good, the bad, and the just plain ugly.

Witness to Crime

Unfortunately, this is one of the risks of living in a city. Crimes tend to occur more often in urban areas, and chances are good that you will one day see a crime in progress. You may be walking home after a nice evening with friends at a local tavern and see a woman being mugged. Or a man urinating in the street. Or a flasher. What do you do?

If It's a Mugger, Get to Safety

1. Unless you're huge and buff and know karate, you do not want to confront a mugger or any other kind of violent attacker. You never know whether a gun or knife may be involved.

2. If you're on a secluded street and there's no one else walking nearby, duck into the nearest safe place,

whether it's an alley or a store or a recessed doorway.

3.   If you have a cell phone, great—this is what they're good for. Call 911. If you don't have a cell phone, get to the nearest pay phone or ask to use the phone in a nearby store or restaurant.

4.   If the attack is taking place in a more populated area, get to safety and then make some noise: Scream, raise a fuss, do whatever you can to attract the attention of passersby. This will also distract the attacker and let him know that he's being observed.

5.   Once the attacker takes off, immediately approach the victim to determine whether he or she is all right.

6.   Remain with the victim at the scene of the crime until the police arrive.

If It's a Urinator or Flasher, Do Nothing

Public urinators and flashers are not as dangerous as muggers. The urinator may have grown up in a barn and have no knowledge of basic socially acceptable behavior, but it's not your job to correct this shortcoming. Just keep quiet and walk past. If you do call attention to yourself, he may turn around while he's still urinating and . . . the result will not be pleasant.

If you are flashed, the most important thing to do is remain blasé. Flashers are looking for a reaction, and if you don't give him one, he won't derive as much pleasure from his lewd act. Do call 911, however. Your description may help the police find the flasher and prevent him from harassing others.

Negotiating the Sidewalk

There is a rhythm and flow to sidewalk traffic in the big city. Generally, it's dictated by the timing of traffic lights, the time of day (rush hour or nighttime), and the day of the week (you'll find more amblers on the weekend than on a weekday). No longer the sole domain of pedestrians, sidewalks today are witness to any number of delicate negotiations: among pedestrians, between pedestrians and People on Wheels (POWs), among hordes of umbrella-wielding walkers determined to stay dry at all costs.

Pedestrian Traffic

The rules of the sidewalk are essentially the same whatever the time of day.

1. Pedestrians should keep to the right at all times, except when passing.

2. Pedestrians have the right to pass other pedestrians at any time, particularly anyone falling under the category of a "slow walker." (See below.)

3. While passing, the pedestrian must always yield to (i.e., step to the right for) oncoming pedestrians traveling in the opposite direction.

4. When stopping to look for something in a bag or examine an item in the window of a store, the pedestrian should sidle up to the nearest right-hand side wall to let other people pass without having to break momentum.

5. Pedestrians should try to maintain the average walking speed of the sidewalk they're traversing.

6. Pedestrians must obey all traffic signs.

7. By law, motorists should yield to pedestrians in a crosswalk; however, pedestrians must always be alert to motorists who flout the law and plow into the intersection.

Contending with Slow Walkers

In a city, the slow-walking clusters are usually made up of tourists and other out-of-towners. More concerned with seeing the sights, marveling at buildings you've never noticed, and ambling at a speed your grandmother would be comfortable with, these pedestrians get in the way of the smooth flow of everyday traffic. When you need to get to a destination quickly, the following techniques have proven to be effective, particularly when faced with a large group of dawdlers.

1.   Resolve to pass the slow walkers—and soon—before you combust from frustration.

2.   Begin to make your presence known by walking close to the group and frequently clearing your throat.

3.   Identify the path of least resistance. Target the "weak link" walker—the one who's walking just a little farther away from the group, leaving a gap just large enough for you to slip through.

4.   Prefacing your actions with a loud "Excuse me," stride forcefully into the gap.

5.   Continue on your way.

People on Wheels (POWs)

You're rounding a corner and something whirs around you

from the opposite direction—it's a bicyclist—and you nearly collide. Sound familiar? How about the rollerbladers on the sidewalk who zoom along until they hit a crack and then swerve or teeter as if they're about to wipe out? Think of how much faster a person on wheels is going than the average pedestrian. The bottom line: It's sometimes dangerous for POWs to be on the same sidewalk with pedestrians. Some towns have ordinances that outlaw riding on the sidewalk, and some even enforce such laws, but the majority of places do not.

When hazarding it out on the sidewalk—by whatever wheeled conveyance you choose—you should be aware of the rules of the walkways. If you set a good example, chances are others will follow suit.

1. Take a lesson or two before you take to the sidewalk— knowing what you're doing will make you less of a nuisance to pedestrians.

2. Wear a helmet.

3. Remember that you are sharing the sidewalk with pedestrians: Always be aware of where they are in relation to you.

4.   Keep in mind that you are going faster than the average pedestrian; thus you will be the one to inflict damage in a collision.

5.   Do not deviate from a predictable, straight course. That will allow pedestrians and other POWs to move aside or around your position accordingly.

6.   Always pass on the left.

7.   Equip yourself or your vehicle with a subtle but effective noisemaking device (e.g., a regular horn, not a foghorn) so that you can alert pedestrians when you are behind them and need to pass. Alternatively, when coming up on pedestrians or other POWs, call out your position—"on your left" or "on your right"—to alert them that you are about to pass.

8.   Be sure to slow down as you pass so that you are prepared to stop quickly and safely if need be.

9.   Slow down when rounding corners, and always make a wide arc, rather than hugging the wall, so that anyone rounding the corner in the other direction will see you in time to move.

10. Take up as little space as possible—you're already cutting a larger figure on your wheels than the average pedestrian. Lock your arms and elbows to your sides, keeping as narrow a profile as possible.

11. Yield to the elderly, to children, and to adults walking with children.

Rain Rage and Umbrella Etiquette

Some people carry umbrellas big enough for a family of five. When you try to pass them on the sidewalk with your properly sized one-person umbrella, they play "umbrella chicken" and force you to move aside and let them pass. Others wield their folded-up umbrellas with reckless abandon, blissfully unaware that they nearly poked out your eye with their tip while boarding the bus.

According to etiquette experts, incidents like these have given rise to a phenomenon known as "rain rage": the seething, bile-in-the-throat reaction one experiences on rainy days when fellow pedestrians, unaware of the proper way to share the space and keep dry, persist in violating others' personal space with their umbrellas.

No one likes getting wet as they rush to and from the workplace, the bus stop, or the car, but there are certain rules one can follow that allow everyone to stay dry.

1.   Hold the umbrella high enough so that you can see not only where you're walking but also who is walking toward you, thus avoiding collisions.

2.   When walking beneath a scaffold where you're sheltered from the rain, close your umbrella. These spaces are often tight, and people can't easily fit through if everyone's umbrellas are open.

3.   If you're approaching someone on the street who is taller than you, lower your umbrella to leave sufficient room for the approaching umbrella to pass overhead.

4.   If you are taller than the pedestrian approaching, lift your umbrella so that it passes over the other without collision.

5.   If the person approaching happens to be your same height, try to negotiate. Make eye contact. Say, "I'm moving to the right" or "I'm moving to the left"— whichever makes the most sense based on your position. When she moves in the opposite direction, you can pass each other without incident.

ETIQUETTE TIPS

When taking public transportation:

- Don't shake your umbrella on anyone in a subway car or on a bus.
- While closing your umbrella, make sure the pointed end faces away from other passengers.
- Rest your wet umbrella on the floor, not on a seat other passengers will use.

Revolving-Door Etiquette

Revolving doors are a common feature in urban buildings that contain many floors of office workers. Designed to prevent large gusts of air conditioning or heat from escaping when doors are constantly opened and closed and to regulate an efficient flow of people in and out of the building, revolving doors carry their own rules.

1. Only one person at a time may enter each wedge of a revolving door.

2. When going through a revolving door, do not push too aggressively—your pace may be too fast for people occupying the other sections.

3. Use the handle provided to push the door—do not smudge the glass with your hands.

4. If you see someone entering from the other side at the same time as you, pause to let that person board first.

5. If you're uncertain you'll make it into a particular wedge, don't risk it—wait patiently for the next one to come around, as it surely will.

ETIQUETTE TIP
If you have luggage or any other kind of large load with you, avoid using revolving doors altogether. It will be nearly impossible to maneuver the door and cumbersome packages—unless, of course, the door revolves automatically.

APARTMENT LIVING

With thin walls, poor ventilation, and tiny living spaces, city apartment buildings are breeding grounds for misbehavior. Whenever people live in close quarters, interpersonal clashes are inevitable.

Crowded Elevator Protocol

The apartment building elevator is one place where all of our notions of personal space are sure to be violated—it's a regular human incubator. There you are, packed in like sardines, with strangers breathing down your neck and bumping up against you. All the while, everyone stares straight ahead or down at the floor, trying to pretend they're not where they are, just holding their breath and gritting their teeth until that little metal box stops at their floor.

There is much potential for incivility here: someone could touch you or sneeze on you; you could miss your floor because the elevator was too crowded for you to push your button or you're squashed into the corner and didn't make it out in time. The high degree of discomfort prevents people from acting kindly—their goal is simply to get out and forget the people they treat rudely along the way.

Following some basic rules of elevator etiquette will make this a more civil environment from the outset.

1. Always let disembarking passengers exit before you enter an elevator.

2. Once inside, briskly push the button for your floor, move to the rearmost empty spot, and face the doors.

3.   If the only spot happens to be right up front, facing the panel of buttons, it's your duty, when asked, to push riders' floor buttons for them.

4.   If you see someone racing to get on, push the "Door Open" button so he can safely board (unless of course the elevator is full).

5.   If you absolutely must sneeze or cough or clear your throat during the ride, make sure to completely cover all bodily orifices out of which phlegm might escape.

6.   Make room for people who are leaving the elevator, even if it means you, too, must exit the elevator and then reboard.

What happens, though, when the elevator becomes so completely crowded that you're in danger of not being able to exit when it gets to your floor? Ding! The doors open and you say, "Excuse me," as you move forward to exit. But before you can leave, someone else boards and stands in your way.

1.   Utter an extra "Excuse me!"—and another if you must—to make it clear that you are trying to exit.

2.   Say, "I'm getting out on this floor," in an urgent, force-ful manner so that everyone onboard hears you.

3.   If your exit remains blocked, make physical contact, touching people on the shoulders and elbows so that they know you are trying to maneuver your way out the door.

4.   If the doors start to close, appeal to the person closest to the panel to keep the doors open until you pass through.

Dealing with Excessively Noisy Neighbors

It's been determined by academics with a whole lot of time on their hands (specifically, at Northwestern University) that the noise that makes people cringe most is the sound of finger-nails on a blackboard. The second most annoying noise is the sound of two pieces of Styrofoam being rubbed together. Al-though these are certainly irritating in the short term, much more disturbing over the long term is the unremittingly noisy neighbor, particularly in the close quarters of a big-city apart-ment building. Whether she decides to blast her disco compi-lation from 11:15 p.m. to 11:45 p.m. every night, or she has one of those little yappy dogs that refuses to shut up, her thoughtlessness disturbs your tranquility and peace of mind.

How do you maintain your home as your refuge?

A quick review of the basic rules for apartment dwellers is in order.

1. Most apartment buildings have restrictions on how late tenants can play their music. A good rule of thumb is no loud music after 10 p.m. on weeknights and after 11 p.m. on weekends.

2. If you plan to exercise in your apartment, notify the person living below that you're about to jump around a lot and to please let you know if you're too noisy.

3. Be similarly proactive if you're planning a party. Slip invites under the doors of your neighbors to let them know (a) that there will be strangers coming in and out of the building, and (b) that you'll be making more noise than usual that night.

4. If you have a loud pet, do whatever it takes to keep it quiet. (See page 106.)

Confronting a Noisy Neighbor

Of course, just because you're following these Good Neighbor rules doesn't mean your neighbors are. How do you deal with a neighbor who's keeping you up at night?

1.   Shuffle on over to your neighbor's, wearing pajamas and a sleepy expression.

2.   You'll probably need to knock twice since the noise emitting from your neighbor's apartment is so heart-thumpingly loud.

3.   When your neighbor opens the door, you'll need to shout over the racket: "Please, could you turn down the music/muzzle your yappy dog? I'm trying to get some sleep."

4.   Should your request not do the trick, you should notify your apartment super or landlord of your neighbor's thoughtlessness. A quick call from a person in authority may prove a tad more effective than your direct request.

5.   If all else fails, bring in the professionals. Call the cops. If it's after 11:00 p.m., you have every right to complain about excessive noise. Make your phone call and then listen for the sweet sound of silence once those men and women in blue knock on your annoying neighbor's door.

6.   Repeat as necessary. Annoying Neighbor should get the point.

Owning a City-Dwelling Dog

He's at it all day and night: Ruff! Ruff! Grrrrrr. Ruff! Awooooo! His bark is loud and constant and sometimes punctuated by ear-splitting howls. He's upsetting you, not to mention your neighbor's cat, a perfectly civilized being who keeps to himself, bothers no one, and is now on anti-anxiety medication. What to do with your noisy mutt? You already feel guilty for keeping him in your postage-stamp-sized yard.

Having a dog—especially a large one—in the city is difficult, given the lack of space for Fido to romp and stretch his legs. No wonder he gets upset and howls or barks all night. To maintain your sanity, not to mention that of your neighbors, be sure to take your dog out for regular, rigorous exercise and follow these city-pet-owner rules.

1.   Always scoop that poop.

2.   Do not let your mutt poop freely on anyone else's property, especially while said property owner is trying to enjoy his tiny patch of green space or concrete stoop.

3.   When walking your dog, keep him on a relatively short leash so he doesn't cut people off or make them walk in a wide arc to humor his meandering.

4.   Consult your vet for ways to keep your dog quiet at night, even if it involves late-night or early-morning walks or keeping it in a room where it won't disturb others.

5.   Do not bring your dog to the dog park if he has any kind of contagious infections (e.g., pinkeye or fleas).

6.   Consult with your vet about when it's safe to bring him back into the company of other dogs.

7.   If your dog is male, supervise him at all times to make sure he's not mounting and upsetting unwilling females and their owners.

The Front-Door Loiterer

What do you do when there's a stranger standing outside the security door of your apartment building?

It's questionable whether or not this stranger knows someone in the building—but she's standing beside the panel of buzzers as if she's just buzzed a friend's apartment. Would it be polite to just let her walk in with you so she doesn't have to wait?

Uh, no. As a tenant, it's your duty (and in your own best interest) to maintain the security of the building, and that means not letting in strangers just because they appear to be harmless.

The stranger may seem slight and meek, but she could very well be a black belt or someone casing your building for future burglary or other nefarious purposes.

1.   Walk up to the door confidently, acknowledging her with a smile or nod.

2.   Take out your keys, feigning nonchalance with a whistle, and unlock the door.

3.   Open the door only a few inches, or however much would allow only you to fit through.

4.   Quickly pull the door completely closed and make sure it's securely locked.

5.   If she's staring at you strangely while you get your mail from your box in the lobby, simply ignore her and proceed on your way.

ETIQUETTE TIP

When faced with a situation in which you need to express confidence, body language cues are helpful. Walk briskly and hold yourself erect, with your shoulders back. If you stop to talk to someone, stand with your legs apart and your hands on your hips, squarely facing whomever you're speaking to. If you're sitting, cross your legs and clasp your hands behind your head to show confidence and superiority.

Laundromat Etiquette

So many offenses occur at the Laundromat. People walk in already in a bad mood—no one wants to be there—and they take it out on others by removing hapless customers' soaking-wet clothes from washers or their still-damp garments from dryers. Then they leave them in a soggy pile on a folding table that's covered with dryer lint. They hoard machines and jealously guard their rolly carts. They rarely engage in conversation with anyone around them.

It doesn't have to be this way. If only all self-service laundry denizens would follow these essential rules of Laundromat etiquette, the world would be a better place—or at least a cleaner, happier one.

1.   Always stay in the Laundromat while your clothes are

washing or drying so that you can remove them as soon as they're done, thereby immediately freeing the machine for other customers (who would otherwise sit, staring resentfully at your unmoving clothes).

2.   If for some reason you can't stay on the premises, be sure to carefully time your return to coincide with the end of the washing or drying cycle.

3.   If the Laundromat is busy and rolly carts are few, use yours sparingly—just to transport clothes from one machine to another, for example, and not to store your clothes while you're folding.

4.   Do not remove another customer's clothes from a washer that's finished its cycle.

5.   If all of the dryers are full and one of them has been sitting idle for five minutes, you may open the dryer door to check whether the clothes are dry. If they are, remove them and set them in a neat pile on a clean countertop. If they're still wet, they should not be removed.

ETIQUETTE TIP

At any given time, Laundromats develop a kind of temporary community of strangers, each of whom is aware of what his or her fellow launderer is doing. Should you, through no fault of your own, find yourself on the receiving end of a Laundromat violation (e.g., your wet clothes have been unceremoniously dumped out of the washer), the unspoken rule is that you get first dibs on the next available dryer.

CHAPTER 4

LEISURE TIME

It's no wonder that gym memberships have skyrocketed and more and more people are looking for new ways to unwind and reduce stress. Inevitably, though, the process of destressing can become stressful itself when space is at a premium: a thoughtless shopper has left her cart in the middle of the supermarket aisle; a department store denizen is monopolizing the bargain rack; your precious spot on the beach is invaded by unruly children; your place on the stationary bike has been befouled by a sweaty workout fanatic; and so on. Knowing the basic rules of etiquette and learning to deal with etiquette lapses are your best survival tools.

SHOPPING

Whereas some find shopping—be it in the supermarket or the department store—a tiresome chore, others find endless pleasure trolling the aisles, searching for favorite foodstuffs, or rubbing elbows with bargain shoppers on opening day of the big department store sales. Whether shopping is one of your favorite leisure activities or your most hated task, chances are high that you'll be faced with a laundry list of transgressions along the way, from the person who does not comprehend the simple rules of shopping cart navigation to the pesky perfume spritzers who simply won't give up.

Shopping Cart Navigation

Fortunately, your modern supermarket is set up precisely to make navigating its aisles logical and easy. With your shopping cart safely in hand, you can begin to stalk your quarry.

The rules of the supermarket aisle are similar to the rules of the road when it comes to shopping cart navigation.

1.   Keep two hands on the cart at all times when the cart is in motion.

2.   Keep to the center of the aisle when pushing the cart.

3.   Park the cart to the side of the aisle, as close to the shelves as possible, when you pause to pick up a food item.

4.   At the end of an aisle, look both ways before proceeding to the left, right, or forward.

5.   If backing up becomes necessary, be sure to look behind you before entering the maneuver to ensure that the coast is clear.

6.   When turning, move your cart in a firm arc, saying, "Excuse me," as needed so that your intentions are clear to the shoppers around you.

7.   Cart drivers entering a lane from the right have the right of way; drivers in the lane must yield to oncoming traffic.

8.   Unattended carts may be moved to allow for traffic flow.

Delays and obstacles are inevitable at the market, even on a good day. But so long as you keep to the rules, you should be able to get what you need in a prompt and efficient manner.

Say, for example, you've spotted your favorite water crackers about three-quarters of the way down the aisle. You make your way toward the cracker aisle, but halfway down, a blockade halts your progress. It's two stopped carts, and their owners are on separate sides of the aisle. One cart belongs to a young father who is trying to discipline the spastic toddler wedged into his cart's baby seat. He's parked close to one wall of grocery shelves. The other cart, carelessly perched on the diagonal in the center of the aisle, seems abandoned but could belong to either of the two women farther down the aisle who are lifting cereal boxes off the shelves to look at each type's nutritional information.

There isn't enough space for you to maneuver through, so you must move the unattended cart yourself.

1. First, park your own cart to one side of the aisle, behind the cart that belongs to the discombobulated dad.

2. Now, walk over to the unclaimed cart and take hold of the handle with both hands so you can more easily steer it.

3. Quickly push the cart toward the side of the aisle so that there's still plenty of maneuvering space for both you and the man in front of you.

4. Proceed to push your cart through the aisle.

The Impostor in the Express Lane

God bless the innovative thinker who surveyed the super-market checkout lines one day and decided to invent the Express Lane. The Express Lane (its only requirement being that you have fewer than a certain number of items in your shopping cart) lets you pop in and buy your spur-of-the-moment ice cream, the Sunday paper, or that quick bag of ice just before you head out to your afternoon picnic. And the rules of the lane are refreshingly simple.

"

1.   Multiple quantities of the same item do not count as a single item.

2.   Just because something is small—say, a single lemon—doesn't mean it doesn't count as an item.

3.   No exceptions to the rules will be made under any circumstances.

But what about the joker who thinks he can get away with 11, or even—prepare yourself, this is shocking—12 items, even though the lane sign distinctly says "10 Items or Fewer"? Did he fail to pay attention, or is he just trying to pull a fast one on all of the other obedient, rule-abiding shoppers?

It is your duty, on behalf of all the other patiently waiting, coupon-holding patrons throughout the store, to call this offender's bluff.

1.   At the outset, make sure you've counted the items in his basket correctly.

2.   Once you're sure there are more than 10, tap him on the shoulder.

3.   Give him a way out. Point at the sign that specifies the maximum. He may feign surprise and graciously retreat.

4.   If he insists on staying in line, however, point to his basket and say, "It looks like you have more than 10 items."

5.   Now proceed to count out loud the number of groceries in his basket: "A lemon, one; a head of broccoli, two; box of cereal, three . . ." He won't be able to deny it when you pass the 11 mark. By this time, you'll have the rest of the express lane members on your side—a mob mentality never hurts.

Department Store Sales and Bargain Shopping

Now that you've just spent hundreds of dollars at the grocery store, leaving you with a seriously depleted bank account, it's time to tempt fate and head over to the department store for some quick bargain shopping.

First, be happy you're not looking for a wedding dress. Women's faces have been trampled into the wall-to-wall carpeting at Filene's Basement's famous bridal gown blowouts. Bargain shoppers are aggressive, but not as vicious as brides-to-be.

Now that you have the silver lining, let's face it: Bargain shopping is a sport, like shooting clay pigeons, though not as regional, or hockey, though with more contact and no (official) rules.

The *unofficial* rules of bargain-day shopping are:

1.   Kicking, shoving, biting, and hair-pulling are strictly forbidden.

2.   Whoever is the first to lay a hand on the item gets first crack at it.

3.   While two people are looking at a rack of clothing, it's considered rude to push the clothes so that the second person has a harder time seeing the clothes in front of her.

4.   Hiding items in racks where they don't belong so you can come back for them later is cheating.

ETIQUETTE TIP

Keep in mind that other shoppers may not have the best intentions when they tell you how something you're trying on looks. "That makes you look hippy" may simply mean they want you to release custody of it so they can try it on and claim it for themselves.

The skills you need on the day of a big department store sale are focus (knowing what you're looking for); two strong elbows; a mantra; and, in the face of competition over an item, a no-mercy attitude. Should you and another shopper simultaneously lay your hands on the same item of marked-down clothing, be aggressive.

1.   Steel yourself. You can tell just by looking her in the eye that there's no way she's letting go of this cocktail dress marked down from $450 to $180.

2.   Repeat your mantra to yourself—"It *will* be mine. It *will* be mine. It *will* be mine."

3. Give the item a little tug in your direction to test her. She may let go, not wanting to put up a fight.

4. If she responds with a tug of her own, it's time to act. While taking care not to wrinkle or tear the garment, begin to pull it toward your body, locking your elbows close to your chest for extra leverage.

5. Create some sort of distraction ("Look! There's Brad Pitt!" or "Oh, no, there's a hole in the sleeve") so she loses her focus and her grip.

6. Once victory is yours and the dress is safely in your arms, turn and quickly walk in the other direction to avoid further confrontation.

Dealing with Perfume Spritzers

They're in every department store, and sometimes they won't take no for an answer. "Would you like to try some Charlie?" Spritz. "Would you like to try the new fragrance from blah blah designer, Infatuation?" Spritz. Do they ever consider that not everyone likes to smell as if they're obsessed, wear white diamonds, and vacation on the Rive Gauche? You have every right to reprimand the spritzer. Say, "Excuse me, I did not ask to be spritzed with [insert perfume name here]. I am enraged and disgusted." This will effectively create a scene other shoppers will be drawn to, thereby sabotaging any sales the perfume spritzer may have made.

Escalator Etiquette

There are two theories behind how escalators were meant to be used. Some believe they were invented purely to give shoppers and pedestrians a break from incessant walking, and that, once on a moving staircase, you should relax, stand still, give your legs a break, and enjoy the ride. But others see the escalator—and its cousin, the moving walkway—simply as a means to get where they're going more quickly. These people tend to walk the moving stairs or even take advantage of the escalator's momentum by sprinting to the top or bottom.

These two escalator-riding types are often on a collision course at the mall or department store: for example, when the latter is in a hurry but his path is blocked by two riders standing side by side, chatting casually; or when the former is taking a breather, having lugged her shopping bags all over the mall, only to have her reverie interrupted by a jolt from a passing stair sprinter.

But if both types of riders simply obeyed the following rules of escalator etiquette, neither would have reason to resort to rudeness, and both would achieve their goals.

1.   Always stand right, walk left.

2.   Always hold the handrail.

3.   When conversing with a friend on an escalator, stand one step above or below your friend, as opposed to side by side.

4.   If you have heavy bags and you'd like to put them down on the escalator steps, do not place them beside you; instead, use the step above or below your own. Always keep a space free for those who want to walk up or down on the left, and always keep your hand on your bags in case you need to move them quickly.

5.   If you choose to walk, be sure not to jostle any standing riders, and let them know you're coming by uttering a polite "excuse me" as soon as you're within earshot.

6.   If you are standing but decide you'd rather walk, wait until those who are already walking have passed before switching over to the left side.

7.   Whenever possible, keep one to two escalator steps between you and the next passenger.

8.　　Never run on the escalator.

9.　　Never go up the down escalator or vice versa.

Occasionally, you'll run into a pair or trio of riders who aren't familiar with the "stand right, walk left" rule and who are blocking your path. Should you inform them of the rule, or simply ask them to move aside?

Since you are in a hurry, it's best not to engage in what may turn into a lengthy exchange ("What? I've never heard of that rule before . . ."). If your initial "excuse me" does not suffice, add an "Excuse me, I'm trying to get by, I have a [bus/train/end-of-season-sale] I need to catch." Then simply squeeze past as best you can.

ENTERTAINING

Whether you're planning an intimate party for two or a sit-down dinner for 20, every foray into the world of entertaining begins with the most mundane of tasks: planning a menu.

Would that it were all so simple! Along the way you'll have to prepare yourself for the joys of hosting, from pleasing palates to dealing with the guest who can't tell when one more drink is one too many.

Menu Planning

Yeah, we all know about those darn vegans. They're even worse than vegetarians. And you can never be sure when someone's a fishetarian, or if they eat chicken but not red meat. Then there are those people who just won't eat their veggies. Not to mention the different kinds of food allergies—shellfish, legumes, wheat—and the heart patients whose doctors have them furiously watching their cholesterol. How's anyone supposed to plan a successful dinner party these days?

The quickest, most direct, and relatively painless solution: Send out a questionnaire to all your guests before you plan the menu. That's what really hoity-toity bed-and-breakfasts do to make sure they don't cause any of their guests to go into anaphylactic shock.

1. Thanks to the Internet, this task is relatively easy to accomplish—simply e-mail or fax the questionnaire to each of your guests.

2. Include detailed questions about food allergies and individual likes and dislikes.

3. Ask them to list any and all foods that they "absolutely won't eat."

4. Give them a deadline for getting their answers back to you.

5. Inform them that guests who miss the deadline come to the party at their own risk.

If you're not certain you can accommodate a guest's special needs, simply contact him and tell him so; you should be able to work out a satisfactory solution. (Perhaps he could even bring his own specially made dish, and you can reheat it along with your meal.)

Keep in mind that some of your guests may have particular dietary restrictions based on religious beliefs. Those keeping kosher, for example, would not mix dairy and meat at a meal.

ETIQUETTE TIP

So, one of your guests shows up without an RSVP. She says she's allergic to legumes, and you've concocted an all-bean dinner. Even the salad has chickpeas in it. You thought you were golden—you'd satisfied all the vegan/vegetarian combos—but you hadn't thought of this. There's nothing else in your kitchen except a stack of take-out menus. Work fast: Give the allergic guest the stack to choose from, and hold off on serving the meal until her dinner arrives.

Unfortunate Gift Giving

You've made your meal, you've showered and dressed—now it's time for your guests to arrive. It's also time to remember that essential truism: Entertaining, whether at home or elsewhere, puts you in the social sphere where, typically, a lot of lying is involved. "Oh, this gift is perfect!" "I just love these beef cheeks." "You look wonderful!" It's expected of you, and perfectly okay, to fib in these situations. The challenge comes in pulling it off without batting an eye.

"Oh, it's just what I needed, a . . . a . . . what exactly is it?" Bizarre kitchen devices you can't figure out how to use; ugly sweaters, brooches, scarves; ceramic animals that will just collect dust; that dancing, pelvic-thrusting Santa; that damn singing bass—the list goes on and on. It's a fact of life: Some people—even close friends and family members—have really bad taste, so they give really bad gifts.

The simple solution: Return it.

1. Once you open the gift and see that it's heinous or impractical, exclaim how wonderful it is and ask the giver where he got it and how recently, because you want to get one just like it for your sister's birthday.

2. Do not remove any of the packaging—leave the shrinkwrap, the original tag, and box sealant intact.

3.   Armed with the information you so subtly acquired in step 1, return the gift to the store from which it was purchased. Even without a gift receipt, stores will usually take back an item that obviously wasn't opened.

4.   The gift-giver may ask about the gift: "Oh, have you been listening to the singing bass?" Just grit your teeth and lie: "I love it! I can't get the song out of my head!"

A slightly more complex solution to the dilemma is known as "The Regift." This solution works especially well if you're invited to a party by someone you particularly dislike (but you need to attend for the sake of appearances). Simply rewrap the gift in especially nice paper, with ribbon (to compensate for the fact that it's a crappy gift), and present it to your host. Eventually, the gift will be regifted enough times that it will make its way to someone who actually likes it.

When You Can't Return It and It's Too Horrendous to Regift: The Ugly Gift Party

Turn unfortunate gifts into a fun and kitschy evening by throwing an "ugly gift party." Ask guests to wrap and bring the worst gifts they've ever received. Pile the presents in the center of the room. Then have everyone pick a number out of a hat. The person with the highest number chooses first from the pile. Once the game is under way, players can use their turn to take away a present from someone who's already had a turn. Watch the silliness ensue as present after present gets unwrapped and groaned over.

The Guest Who's Had Too Much to Drink

The signs are many: She's slurring her words; she stumbles while trying to cross the room; she's going to the bathroom a lot; she's flirting aggressively with a man she's heretofore described as "totally gross." She is the picture of the sloshed party guest, and if she happens to show up at your party, it's your duty as host to control the situation before she makes a complete fool of herself—or ruins your new Himalayan rug.

The best solution, and the most responsible one, is to get her out—fast. This is most easily accomplished when the guest has come with someone else, so you can transfer responsibility for her to her friend.

1.   Pull the friend aside discreetly: "Listen, don't you think Mary's had a little too much to drink?" Float the suggestion that he take her home.

2.   If she came to the party solo, call her a cab and then ask her to come outside with you for a smoke—or, if she doesn't smoke, to see the moon.

3.   Tell her to bring her coat, because it's chilly out, and her purse, in case the ice cream man drives by.

4.   When the cab pulls up, put her in the backseat, give the driver her address, and place cab fare in her hand. In her state, she's unlikely to put up a fuss.

AT THE GYM

The gym is a place where people are forced to be more intimate with strangers than they would ever choose to be. First of all, there's the wardrobe—did you ever think you'd see your neighbor or coworker in a sports bra and Lycra shorts? Combine that with the fact that she and countless others are using the same machines, mats, and weights as you—and sweating profusely onto them.

In this section we'll explore etiquette in the sweaty netherworld of your neighborhood gym. From sweat spreading to thoughtless channel changing, there are many ways to behave badly in this particular public forum. You need to know how to comport yourself.

Sweatiquette

Maybe you don't go to the kind of gym that has a towel service, but that's never an excuse not to wipe off the machine you just dripped sweat onto for 25 cardio-busting minutes. When it comes to working out, there are a few golden rules regarding sweat and sharing equipment—some are unspoken, other are set by management.

1. Wipe off your sweat. Many gyms provide paper towels and spray disinfectant. This is ideal. The next best option is using a towel and water from your water bottle.

2. If it's a seated machine, you're more likely to produce actual puddles. Don't just quickly wipe these off—hold the towel in place for several seconds to soak up the reservoir of fluid.

3. If you sweat particularly profusely—so much so it's likely to fly off your brow and travel far enough to splash a fellow cardio-buster—choose a machine that's not near any others in use.

Let's say you're about to mount a machine when all of a sudden you spot little puddles of sweat on the handles, the backrest, and—horror of horrors—the seat. Yech, crotch sweat! Clearly, someone has violated rule no. 2. What do you do? The options are twofold: you'll need to either wipe it up yourself or have the sweat spreader do the job.

The proactive solution:

1. Find a box of tissues or a roll of paper towels and at-tack those rank puddles yourself. The person who used the machine before you didn't have the courtesy to do it, but you certainly do—and in doing so you're showing all your fellow gym-goers that keeping the equipment clean is everyone's job.

2. Apply a wad of tissues or paper towels to each puddle of sweat and let it rest there for a few seconds to soak up the moisture.

3. Wipe the rest away using small circular motions. When you catch the eyes of fellow gym-goers, let them know that you're cleaning up after a rampant sweat spreader (a roll of the eyes should do it) so they can be on their guard.

The confrontational solution:

1. Chances are you know exactly whose sweat it is that's befouling the machine you're about to use, since you've been waiting your turn. Track the sweat-spreader to the

spot she's now occupying: the mats? the weights? Take a quick look around to discover her location.

2.   Once you've spotted her, lay your towel on the machine to make sure no one slips onto it while you're confronting the sweat-spreader. Then make your way over.

3.   Point to the machine she just vacated and ask, "Weren't you just using that machine?"

4.   When she says yes, say, "You probably didn't notice that it's really wet. Would you mind wiping it off before the next person uses it?"

5.   If she hesitates, remind her, "It's a gym rule." Then tilt your head toward one of the gym employees manning the floor as if to suggest that you'll have to tell one of them if she doesn't do as you've requested.

Machine Etiquette

"The maximum time limit for cardiovascular machines is 25 minutes during peak hours." That's what the signs say, and they're difficult to miss, hung at regular intervals above the treadmills, StairMasters, and so forth. Yet there are still those self-entitled few who insist on using the machines for 45 minutes, an hour, even longer. They pile their medical textbooks on the digital display and go, go, go, even on a Tuesday at 5:30 p.m., when there are no other unoccupied machines.

All gym-goers should abide by the following common-sense rules so that there are enough machines for everyone:

1. Never hog the machine. The "25-minute rule" is there for a reason: to give everyone a chance.

2. If you're committed to your 45 minutes of cardio, you can still get it in and abide by the rules by cross-training. Run on the treadmill for 25 minutes, then switch over to a StairMaster or bike for the next 20 minutes.

3. If it's peak hours and you see someone waiting for the machine that you've been using for longer than the allotted 25 minutes, begin to cool down and then move on to another machine.

The best approach when someone refuses to play by the rules is confrontation. It may not be a pleasant prospect, but you do have those signs to back you up as well as, undoubtedly, the many unengaged personal trainers and other gym staff who are manning the premises. (Plus, right there on the digital display is proof that this person has exceeded the maximum time limit for peak hours.)

1. Walk right up to the machine hog and say: "Excuse me, how much longer will you be using this machine?"

2. If he is not covering the time window with a towel or magazine, point to it and say: "You've been on this machine for more than 25 minutes."

3. Now that you have his attention, get to the point. Gesture toward the sign explaining the maximum time limit and say, "I'm sorry, but your time is up and I'd like to use this machine now."

4. If he should balk or ignore you, just tap one of those meaty trainers on the shoulder and enlist his help.

ETIQUETTE TIPS

Always set a good example for fellow gym-goers:

- Return weights to their proper resting place, even if you found them strewn all over the floor.
- Allow other people to work in on your machine.
- Do not rest too long between sets on a machine if it looks like people are waiting to use it.

- If you can accommodate someone in any way—by moving over to make room, for instance—do so.
- In exercise classes, be aware of your personal space bubble and do not pierce others' bubbles unless absolutely necessary.

Changing Channels

It's great that gyms have set up "cardio theaters," the marketing world's term for the TVs that hang in a row from the ceiling for the viewing pleasure of those toiling away on gym equipment. Running or climbing stairs in place is especially boring when you're staring at the wall or, worse, yourself. Watching some NBA action or a quality *Golden Girls* rerun can really spice up a workout and, most important, entice you to stay on the machine longer. (It also lets the gym charge even more for a monthly membership.)

Usually, the gym staff has control of the remote, which ensures there's an equal mix of sports, news, and fluff. But members can sometimes ask for channels to be changed. If you're not happy with the selection being shown and would like to watch something else, bear in mind the following:

1.   Others may be watching the same set. Look around to determine who is watching the TV you have chosen.

2. If anyone seems to have their eyes glued to the screen, ask if they'd mind if you changed the channel. They may be staring blankly at it and won't care what's showing.

3. Once you've asked a member of the gym staff for control of the remote, choose a program that won't be objectionable to your gym-mates: no soft porn, *When Animals Attack*, or anything hosted by Joan Rivers.

4. If another gym-goer asks for the remote, graciously give up control.

Observing and Being Observed

Unfortunately, equipment at many gyms—the machines, the weight benches, the mats—is typically placed a little too close together. As a result, it's difficult not to let your eyes wander over to a fellow gym-goer when you're zoning out in a workout daze. You have to remember, though, that people who go to the gym are of different ilks, and some don't like to be observed while they're working out. (And they don't like you checking out the digital display of their machine to see how long and hard they've been exercising.)

Here's a rough sketch of the different gym types:

- The narcissist wears skimpy clothing and has matching workout gear that came in a set. She tends to work out the least, spends a lot of time chatting with other gym members, and preens in the mirror. She wears an unthinkable amount of makeup for someone who is planning to perspire.

- The hardcore exerciser reads a copy of *Fitness*, *Shape*, or *Runner's World*. She's on a first-name basis with the personal trainers and is in scarily good shape. The male equivalent of this is the really well-muscled guy who lives in the weight room and knows all the other heavyweights because they spot for each other all the time.

- The recreational gym-goer comes three or four times a week—if she's wearing Lycra shorts, she's also wearing an oversized T-shirt to hide her butt. She talks to no one except maybe people she already knows from outside the gym. She just gets through her routine and leaves, looking the whole time as if she'd rather be somewhere else.

- The newbie is out of shape and in a slight daze, as if shocked at the existence of this strange world where people voluntarily sweat and exert themselves unnecessarily. He is scrawny and wearing shapeless shorts, an old T-shirt, socks pulled up to his knees, and inappropriate footwear, such as tennis sneakers or loafers.

Each of the above types will react differently when they catch you looking. The narcissist will pose and preen; the hardcore exerciser will be so focused on her heart-rate monitor, she won't even notice. But if the person on the machine or weight bench next to you is a recreational gym-goer or a newbie, he may become uncomfortable.

The best approach is always to keep your eyes on what you're doing, whether it's on the digital display of your machine or your own image while you do bicep curls in the mirror. It's easy to zone out between sets and let your eyes wander. Just make sure they rest in neutral places.

ETIQUETTE TIP

If you do catch someone else's eye by mistake, look away slowly and deliberately—but not too quickly, as that may mislead him into thinking you meant to look in the first place.

When You're Being Checked Out

Some people mistake the gym for a social arena, even a pick-up joint. This is unacceptable (except, of course, if you find the other person extremely attractive). What to do when a gym patron is checking you out and you don't like it?

1.   Do not meet the person's gaze. Resist the temptation to look over to see if she is still looking at you, which could be misread as interest.

2.   If someone approaches you and makes small talk, let that person know you're there to work out, not to be picked up. Say, "Sorry, I need to focus on my workout." Then turn back to what you were doing.

3.   If the person continues to pursue you, become more forceful: "Listen, I really don't come to the gym to meet people. I like to work out and get out as quickly as possible."

Yoga Class Etiquette

Yoga is an excellent mode of relaxation, but not when others in your class are violating your space. This type of gym activity requires even more attentiveness than usual; in order for yoga to be effective, each class member must be able to focus completely on what his or her body is doing.

With that in mind, be sure to review these basic pointers when attending yoga class.

1.   Always make sure you're not taking up more space than you need to. Unless otherwise directed, confine yourself to the limits of your yoga mat (about two by five feet).

2.   Recognize that others may need to encroach on your space from time to time to execute a pose.

3.   Remember that, unless your session calls for it, heavy breathing can be distracting and should be minimized.

4.   When performing a head or shoulder stand, the plough pose, or other extended postures, be sure you have enough space around you so that you do not hit anyone before, during, or after assuming the position.

5.   During quiet meditation and corpse pose (savasana), be sure to refrain from unnecessary chatter.

ON VACATION

What you wanted was to get away from it all—work, the constantly ringing phone, your jammed e-mail inbox. So you looked over some vacation options, with images of piña coladas and long afternoons reading on the beach dancing in your head, only to arrive in paradise and find that it's not so relaxing after all. Instead of worrying about your 9 a.m. staff meeting and that memo from the boss, you're stressed out about what to do with your loud hotel neighbors and those rowdy kids at the beach whose parents have abandoned them (for good reason).

In general, vacationers should employ a do-unto-others approach to interpersonal situations: Never take up too much space on the beach (you wouldn't like your personal space to be encroached upon, would you?); try to keep hotel room noise to a minimum (you wouldn't like your neighbors to overhear your amorous adventures, would you?); and remember that just because nobody here knows you, there's no excuse for misbehavior.

On the Beach

Be sure to follow the basic rules of good behavior when relaxing on the beach.

1.   When settling on a spot to lay your towel and other beachy props, look for a relatively empty stretch of sand. For your own beach pleasure and for those around you, keep at least five feet of beach between your "camp" and the next person's.

2.   Keep your music to yourself, unless you're on a truly deserted beach. If there is just a smattering of people, you can try turning your boom box on low and then test its decibel level by walking over to the nearest person to see if it can be heard from where he's sitting. The best bet, though, is to wear headphones.

3.   With any kinds of games that involve flying objects— Frisbee or Aerobie, Kadima, badminton, etc.—toss only where there's no danger of the object flying into someone's head or picnic lunch.

4.   If you're swimming in the ocean or lake and having fun splashing around with friends and family members, make sure not to encroach upon the space of those you do not know. They may not like to be splashed as much as you do.

5.   If you are European or just very open and you'd like to

sunbathe nude or topless, do so only at a beach that is designated as a nude or topless beach or at a private beach where you the owner has given you verbal consent.

Staking Out a Spot

Keeping in mind rule no. 1 regarding personal space, make sure that you place your belongings no closer than five feet from your nearest neighbor. Ideally, every other beachgoer will follow suit.

But what about those people who bring so much equipment that it takes five trips back and forth from the SUV to fully unload? Tents, giant beach towels, a couple of chairs, some coolers, a volleyball net, rafts, boogie boards, beach balls—they are taking up a huge amount of space. And on this beautiful beach day, it's all you can do to find a two-by-three-foot patch to lay down your modest towel and your solitary backpack filled only with bottles of lotion, water, your MP3 player, some tapes, and a book.

The best approach, as always, is the direct and polite one.

1. First, make sure they're not members of a satanic cult or descendants of Branch Davidians who've decided to build their compound by the sea. Look for telltale pentagram tattoos or any clothing or accessory that can be interpreted as a uniform. Are they all wearing the same

type of Nikes? Are there fewer men than women and an unusually large number of children?

2.   Once you've assessed that they're just a regular, albeit large, family, approach one of the elders.

3.   Be polite when you ask him to move (a) his volleyball net, (b) one of his four tents, or (c) the location of the fire pit they're about to dig, so that you can find a place to lay your towel.

4.   Once he frees up the space, set up your spot and clamp on those headphones to drown out the sounds of all those screaming kids.

Lotion Etiquette

The beach or pool would be better places if we didn't have to put on lotion. It takes so much time to apply, you always miss spots, it gets your hands all greasy and sticky, and you have to reapply every time you go swimming. Then there are the personal space issues involved in sharing lotion and applying it to other people's hard-to-reach areas. Who to ask? And do you really have to reciprocate?

1. If you're with a few companions, ask the one you know best to spread lotion on your back.

2. If you feel like they've missed a spot, let them know.

3. If someone applies your lotion, it's only polite to return the favor.

4. While applying lotion to an acquaintance's back, do so as clinically as possible, with light, short swipes, as opposed to long, languorous, deep strokes.

5. If you have extra lotion on your hands when you're finished applying, don't smear it onto your nearest friend. Just continue to rub it into your skin until it's absorbed.

6. Don't use lotion-spreading as a pick-up line. That's so 1970s.

Lotion Duty and How to Evade It

One day, you may be at the beach with some friends of friends and one of them will nonchalantly ask you to spread lotion on his or her back.

You may already be finished applying your own lotion—you did it at home, in front of the mirror, so you wouldn't miss any spots—and you don't want to get your hands greasy again. Plus, you hardly know this person, and you don't want to be touching a stranger's back. How to gently extricate yourself from the situation?

1.   Review the ingredients list on your own lotion bottle and find a substance that pretty much all lotions share— aloe, PABA, etc.

2.   Ask the person who wishes to be lotioned, "Does your lotion have PABA in it? Because I'm allergic to that."

3.   Let them read the ingredients on the back of the bottle and confirm that the allergen is indeed there.

4.   Apologize for not being able to apply lotion to the unreachable spots, but you would break out in hives if you came into contact with the allergen.

Kids on the Beach

A note to parents: You chose (presumably) to bear these children, and forevermore they'll remain your responsibility. Supervise them at the beach to make sure they're not:

1.   Bothering your beach neighbors by kicking sand in their direction or being noisy, rowdy, or annoying (e.g., throwing objects in their direction).

2.   Splashing water any farther than five feet in any direction.

3.   Playing with dangerous-looking dogs.

4.   Speaking to anyone who may not wish to be spoken to.

When you've been pining for solitude and rest, the last thing you need on vacation is a bunch of unruly kids running around, kicking up sand while you're trying to relax to the more subtle sound of waves crashing on the beach.

When the splashing and kicking get out of control, and appeals to the parents are unsuccessful, try simply scaring them away from your sandy haven. Become that weird adult you used to fear when you were a kid. That involves general unpredictability and certifiably insane behavior. You may want to yell, "Hey kids, what's the capital of Timbuktu?" And then laugh hysterically. Or walk up to one of them and say you're doing a survey on the number of times people swallow in a minute. Once the parents see you, they'll tell their kids to stay clear.

If that doesn't scare them off, try the ice-cream truck fake-out. Look at your watch and say, "Looks like it's just about time for the ice-cream truck! You better go ask your parents for money." They'll clear out in no time.

In the Hotel Room

Many hotels and motels have flimsy walls that are easily penetrated by sound. You never know how thin the walls are until you have a noisy neighbor, so it's always the best policy to keep your voice down and the TV low. Proper hotel-room etiquette dictates that:

1. Televisions, radios, and other devices must be turned down low by 10 p.m.

2. In-room parties should be moved to the lobby by 10 p.m.

3. Guests should refrain from loud conversations after 10 p.m.

4. Guests should refrain from rearranging the furniture in the room.

5. Guests should tip chambermaids at least a dollar a day for every day they've stayed in the room. (And just because you don't have to clean it up doesn't give you license to be messy.)

6.   If you order room service, make yourself presentable when the waiter comes to the door.

For most of us, the rules of proper behavior during a hotel stay are pretty much commonsensical. But every now and then, you may find yourself with the bad luck to be stuck next door to a room that never sleeps. Who knows what they're doing on the other side of that wall? The TV's blaring, people are shouting at one another, and the headboard is knocking against the wall. This is a vacation? You can't even think straight much less get any sleep.

The best solutions:

- Inform the front desk of the problem. Ask to speak with the manager if the clerk on duty says he can't do anything about it. Politely remind the manager that you are a paying customer and expect to be treated as a valued guest.

- Find a blunt instrument in your room—the toilet plunger, a lamp—to knock against the wall. Now knock it sharply against the wall. (This is the universal language for "shut up in there.")

CHAPTER 5

DATING, LOVE, AND SEX

These questions have a way of bringing out people's insecurities—everyone wants to be loved, but there are so many things that can go wrong, and so much potential for misreading and misunderstanding. What follows is a partial road map for the most critical aspects of relationship etiquette, from finding love to letting it go.

Finding Love: The Personal Ad

Frustrated with the usual singles' hangouts? There are alternative ways to meet people. Many publications and websites run personal ads: your local weekly regional magazines, online resources like Match.com or Nerve.com. Figuring out where to place your ad is just the beginning—what should you write, and what do you do when people respond? Some pointers:

1.   Place the ad in the publication or on the website that you read most and that you could see your imaginary intended reading.

2.   Do not place an ad unless you're serious about using it as a means of finding your intended; do not use it as a social experiment.

3.   Don't lie in your ad—no exaggeration of physical traits, intellectual prowess, or jobs held. It might be fine to stretch the truth a bit on a resume, but now you're playing with people's emotions.

4.   Your ad should include your age, your interests, your pet peeves, and what you're seeking in a mate.

5.   Read your ad to a few friends to get their opinions on

whether they think it accurately describes you.

6. If you decide to respond to someone else's ad or make a
    date with one of the people who responds to yours, the
    first meeting should be in a public place and for a lim-
    ited amount of time. Meet for coffee or a drink. If you
    like the person, your next date can be longer and more
    involved, such as dinner and a movie.

First Dates

This is your chance to make a good impression on that person
you've been admiring from afar. Whether you're the inviter
or the invited, keep in mind the following tips.

1. If you're asking a person out on a date, make it clear
    that is what you're asking for—no vague invites that can
    be misconstrued as just two friends hanging out.

2. A first date should have some sense of ceremony or at
    least give the impression that whoever initiated the date
    put some thought into it. It should be planned ahead to
    avoid awkward instances of, "Uh, I don't know, where
    do you want to go?"

3. A good option for a first date is to attend a cultural event, such as a play, movie, or museum. That will give you common neutral ground on which to share observations—plus, choosing this sort of venue has the potential to impress.

4. Avoid restaurants that could get sloppy: no Mexican (leaky fajitas), no sushi (too-large maki hanging out of your mouth), anyplace requiring the use of chopsticks (nervousness could result in a momentary lack of coordination), and places where you eat with your hands (too much potential for spills).

5. Never talk about an ex on a first date (save it for later in your relationship, if it comes to that).

6. Also avoid discussing STDs (presumptuous and a turnoff) and other diseases or afflictions; the intricacies of your family's dysfunctions; any high school awards/honors you won; your financial situation; pets; former marriages; kids; time spent in the Big House.

7. Never assume that your date will foot the bill just because he/she asked you out. Always bring cash just in case (it also comes in handy if you need to make a quick

escape). When the bill arrives, follow the inviter's lead; if it looks like he's going to pay for it all, offer to chip in. He should say no, but it's polite to ask.

First-Date Attire

Most important on a first date is cleanliness and good grooming: no rank body odor, no stray ear or nose hairs or dirt under your fingernails or behind your ears. To attain this goal, you should shower or bathe with a pleasant-smelling soap on the day of your date and use the appropriate tools—razor, nose-hair clipper, tweezers—to rid yourself of errant hairs. Blemishes can be difficult to conceal, but women can try their best with makeup; men should make sure to pop those whiteheads.

Women: Think about the image you want to convey. Many abide by the demure rule when dressing for a first date, that is, nothing too sexy or outlandish that might threaten or intimidate. It's always a good bet to balance a modest outfit with a sexy pair of shoes. But if dressing somewhat conservatively will violate the primary tenets of your individual style, then by all means dress as you always dress, keeping in mind that you may turn off a date who is especially insecure or easily intimidated. Some basics: no cleavage (bosom or butt); don't overdo the makeup or perfume; skirts should fall below the thigh; stick with neutral, flattering colors. Wearing lush, touchable fabrics like mohair, cashmere, or velvet is always a good choice.

Men: With fewer options, choosing what to wear is easier for men—although there are many subtle ways to prompt a visit from the fashion police. Think neutral—a button-down shirt and nice pants or, if it's summer, a polo shirt with nice pants, dark socks, and presentable shoes. Some basics: Don't overdo it on the cologne; clean-shaven is preferred; no chest hair should be showing; save the novelty ties for later (much later); no capris, man-sandals, or man-purses (or, if you prefer, "European carryalls").

When Your Date Is Ex-Obsessed

All through the date she continues to mention him. "My ex, Iggy, hated this restaurant"—followed by a smirk as if she's somehow rebelling against him by coming here. Beware: this kind of behavior shows an unhealthy attachment to an ex. Perhaps she's still trying to show him up and is simply using you as a pawn. If you make it back to her apartment, you might even see framed pictures of Iggy on her bookshelf or, even worse, next to her bed. This date is a complete bust, so you might as well have fun playing therapist.

1.   First, assess the situation. Get some basics—how long ago did she and Iggy break up? Are they still "friends"?

2.   Then clue her in: "You know, Suzie, considering that you and Iggy parted ways more than six months ago, you should really be over him by now, or at least more over him than this."

3.   Tell her what she needs: "You need closure. Maybe you need to hear it from Iggy that it's over for good."

4.   Be considerate and rescue the evenings of other poor fellows like yourself: "Whatever you do, don't go out on any more dates until you're over this guy."

5.   Now get out there and find someone who's not hung up on an ex.

Dealing with a Cheapskate Date

By long-standing custom, the person inviting another out on a date is presumed to be accepting primary responsibility for the tab. Certainly, individuals may choose to decide otherwise, or invitees may wish to pay their share of the bill.

In the absence of any such discussion, however, be aware that when your date talks you out of ordering an appetizer or dessert and steers you toward the second cheapest entrée item on the menu, there's every indication that she's not going to be treating you to a night of fine dining. More likely than not, you're going to be sharing the bill. (It may still be a surprise, however, when she pulls out her calculator and starts tabulating what you owe.) Prepare yourself in advance.

1. Always make sure to have cash on hand for such awkward situations or in case you need to escape early.

2. When the check arrives, let your date take the lead—after all, she's the one who asked you there.

3. If she tabulates what she owes and then asks for your share, there's nothing you can do at this point except pay up.

If this episode leaves a bad taste in your mouth, cut the date short. Tell her you made a previous engagement that you completely forgot about until then.

Alternatively, if you're sure you never want to date the cheapskate again, go ahead and have a little fun at her expense: Once you see it coming—"These appetizers are so overpriced!" and "You know, you really shouldn't drink alcohol. How about some nice ice water?"—start to stack the bill. Appetizer? Oh yes, please, I can never resist shrimp cocktail. Wine? Oh, yes, your finest house white. The lobster looks fabulous tonight. And for dessert, the chocolate soufflé. Watch her eyes begin to bug out and her forehead perspire as she adds up the astronomical bill in her head.

Saying "I Love You"

The "I love you" conundrum. It's different in every situation, yet fundamentally the same. Are you ready to render yourself completely vulnerable to someone by saying "I love you" first, thereby surrendering all of the power, all of "the hand" in the relationship? Do you love this person? What is love, and how do you know when you're in it? Here are some guidelines.

1. If you can help it, avoid saying "I love you" first. This sets the balance for your relationship—and you want to be the one with the power, not the one who's surrendered it completely.

2. Don't say "I love you" just to get sex. That's the height of tackiness.

3. There's a difference between "in love" and "love." Wait to say "I love you" until you're out of the honeymoon, falling-in-love stage (usually the first three months) and into the real relationship—when your blinders are off and you're thinking more clearly.

4.   Don't feel pressured to say "I love you" back if you
     don't really feel it. Wait to return the sentiment until
     you're really sure that you do.

How to Know You Love Someone

1.   Your heart beats faster at the prospect of seeing him or her.

2.   You can see yourself spending, if not the rest of your life,
     then a very long time with him or her.

3.   He or she treats you extremely well, with respect and
     consideration.

4.   You've had your first fight, and you resolved it satisfac-
     torily, through listening and compromising.

5.   He or she makes you laugh.

ETIQUETTE TIP

Saying "I love you" is a sentiment that should be shared in
person—no wimping out and declaring your love via e-mail.

Sex Etiquette

Say your date is successful, lasts well into the night, and is followed by another date and then another. There's no doubt about it: you'll soon be confronting the sticky subject of sex. People have various personal rules about sex. Some have no problem with it on a first date; others will only go so far as a peck on the cheek on a first date. Some have a three-month rule. Some insist that getting it over with sooner is better since you can make a more informed decision about going forward with the relationship.

Confused? Here are some tried-and-true rules.

1.   Never have sex on the first date. You do not know this person well enough to be exchanging bodily fluids.

2.   How far should you go on a first date? No farther than an innocent kiss (no tongue). The exception to this rule is if you were friends with the person before you decided to date and thus have sufficient mutual history.

3.   When should you have sex? If you're under the age of 18: not yet. If you're over 18: when there is the proper amount of affection, attraction, and trust.

4.   Be up-front about whether or not you're ready. If your

partner looks like he is headed toward sex, but you're not ready, make it known explicitly that it will not happen that night.

5.   Before you have sex, be frank with each other about past and present STDs and whether you've been tested for HIV.

6.   Decide what protection you will use and who is responsible for providing it.

ETIQUETTE TIP

After sex at your partner's place, it's prudent to foster togetherness by staying the night. Be a good overnight guest: no hogging the bed or blankets, and no snooping in the medicine cabinet.

The Fetishist

You're a grown-up. You know that some people have fetishes. You just weren't expecting this person to be one of them. What do you do when your mate asks you to do something you're not into?

1.   Take stock of the situation: How much do you like this person? Is it enough to play along once in a while?

2.   Take stock of the fetish. How weird is it? Is it something you could possibly put up with now and again?

3.   If you answered no to the questions in steps 1 and 2, it's time to let this person go. It's not fair to either of you to continue a relationship in which he or she will feel unfulfilled and you'll feel put upon. (See "Breaking Up," below.)

4.   If you answered yes in steps 1 and 2, however hesitantly, tht means you're open to exploration. Let your partner know you'll need to be eased into it. It's possible that you can substitute acts that you are less uncomfortable with for the fetish.

Breaking Up

Let's get the cliché over with up front: Breaking up is hard to do. Okay. Now we can move on. There are many reasons for making the break—some are completely justifiable (she cheated); some are not (he overused emoticons in e-mails). Either way, there are proper ways and improper ways of breaking up. Here are some essential rules.

1.   As always, be up-front about your feelings. Don't try to manipulate the other person into breaking up with you first.

2.   Truly break up with the person—don't just disappear, move to a different state, or change your phone number to avoid confrontation.

3.   Clearly state your reasons, tempering them according to your soon-to-be ex's level of sensitivity.

4.   Indicate what you'd like to happen next so the other person knows exactly what to expect. For example: "I don't think it's realistic for us to try to be friends."

5.   Do it in person, not over the phone, not via a letter, and especially not by e-mail.

Seeking Help: Shrink Etiquette

After any breakup—whether you're the dumper or the dumpee—many of us cast around for whatever means of support can help us through a difficult time. Friends and family will no doubt provide listening and sympathetic ears. But for those times when extra support is needed, a good therapist can be indispensable.

You essentially pay your therapist to be your friend, yet your relationship with him or her is so much different from a friendship. (For one thing, there's that fee; pulling out your checkbook at the end of a tear-drenched session is a pretty harsh reality check.) But what are the rules for choosing a therapist to begin with? How should you negotiate the waiting room? And how do you go about finally breaking up with your shrink?

Here are the basics:

1. Never go to a friend's therapist. If it's unavoidable and you must, make sure you do not discuss your friend during sessions.

2. Do not ask about your therapist's personal life. This is your therapy, and you're paying by the hour.

3. Never lie to get medication.

4. Do cry and scream and fall apart—that's what the tissues and white-noise machines are for.

5. Refrain from scrutinizing other patients in the waiting room or the patient who's leaving as you're coming in. Direct eye contact may make other patients uncomfortable.

6. Don't talk about your sessions to anyone other than close friends or family. (Refrain from starting sentences with "My shrink says . . .")

7. When you feel that you've benefited all you can from therapy, or if you feel that it's not working out, be honest about ending the sessions.

How to Break Up with Your Shrink

At some point, after coming to the shrink regularly and dealing with your "issues," you may feel that it's time to make a go of it on your own. Here's how to end this particular doctor-patient relationship.

1. Decide when your last session will be.

2. A few sessions before your projected last appointment, mention that you want to terminate treatment.

3. Be firm about your decision. If your therapist is good, he or she will respect your wishes and suggest a good way to use your remaining time together.

When Your Shrink Won't Let Go

Maybe he's bleeding clients and money and doesn't want to let his patients leave. Is there desperation in his expression? Is his office becoming messier, his clothes more disheveled? He may be afraid to lose you, in which case he'll try to talk you out of leaving. And it's hard to say no to your therapist—he knows exactly which buttons to press.

1.   Continue to be firm and use phrases like, "I'm confident," "I'm sure," and "I've made up my mind."

2.   If he begins to list the reasons why you should stay, listen to him and then say, "I appreciate your input, but I'm really firm on this decision. We've reached the end."

3.   If the situation becomes uncomfortable, make this session your last. Your shrink obviously doesn't have your best interests in mind, so there's no need to continue.

CHAPTER 6

Out on the Town

Perhaps it's your neighbor at the movie theater who's crinkling candy wrapper after candy wrapper, or the person sitting next to you at a concert who feels compelled to sing along to every song. Perhaps some drunken fool at a bar is trying to pick you up, or your waiter is unspeakably rude. Maybe some people at the next table are eavesdropping on your conversation. Whatever the case, the single most important rule for any entertainment venue is to enjoy yourself without compromising the enjoyment of those around you.

MOVIE THEATER ETIQUETTE

Annoying sounds like wrapper crinkling, loud talking, or loud chewing have no place in the movie theater once the feature is underway. Many theaters go as far as flashing a warning before each movie: "Be considerate of those around you and refrain from unnecessary noise."

To make the movie-going experience as pleasurable as possible, keep in mind the following basic tenets of movie theater etiquette:

1. When choosing a seat, try to make sure you won't be blocking the sight lines of the person behind you. If there are two spare seats available—one in front of and one to the right of a patron—choose the latter.

2. Turn off all electronic media, including personal computers and phones, before the previews.

3. Remember to take off your hat or other item of clothing that might block the view of those around you.

4.   When a theater is crowded, remove your belongings from empty seats to accommodate other patrons.

5.   Open candy wrappers or any noisy packages before the feature film; if you must do so during the movie, remove the wrapper quickly—and preferably during an action sequence.

6.   Refrain from conversation once the movie begins.

7.   If you're eating popcorn, be careful to retrieve it from the bag as gently and as noiselessly as possible. During a quiet scene, try sucking on the popcorn for a few seconds before masticating to minimize the crunching sound.

8.   Do not slurp the very last drops of soda through the straw when you get to the end, and refrain from chewing the ice.

9.   Never bring plastic shopping bags into a theater; if doing so is unavoidable, do not fiddle with the bags during the film.

10. If you've seen the movie more than once, refrain from reciting upcoming dialogue, out of respect for those who

are seeing it for the first time.

11. Do not yell at or in any way attempt to communicate with the characters onscreen.

12. If you're watching a 3-D movie, refrain from swerving in your seat to avoid the special effects. If you find yourself doing so, it's probably a good idea to watch a few 3-D movies at home before doing so in a public movie theater.

Confronting Loud Eaters and Pesky Talkers

Who hasn't been one of these movie theater offenders at one point? Hopefully, someone gave you a pointed glare or a hostile "*Sh!*"—as you should, too, when a person nearby is crunching popcorn too loudly or keeps stage-whispering to a companion, "What did he say?" and "Who is that?" and "What just happened?" Follow these simple steps to make the best of the confrontation.

1. Give a quick glance around to make sure you've correctly identified the offender.

2. Twist your head in his direction.

3.   Fix your eyes on him and tense your eyebrows down-
       ward so that you look stern and schoolmarmish.

4.   Hold your glare for about three seconds.

5.   If he doesn't get the point, repeat steps 2 through 4, but
       add a short "*Sh!*" at the end of step 4. If you don't mind
       escalating the confrontation—and have no fear of con-
       cealed weaponry—you may also choose to say force-
       fully, but politely, in a low voice, "Please keep your voice
       down" or "Stop kicking my seat."

6.   If all else fails, you may have to move to another seat (if
       that's an option) or ask the theater manager or usher to
       confront the culprit.

The Feet-on-Seat Offender

You settle into your seat, arrange your coat on the back of
your chair, stick your cold soda in its holder, and start munch-
ing your popcorn. Life is good: you're about to see a movie
that's been getting great reviews, and this popcorn is nice and
salty and buttery. Then someone has the temerity to slip into the
row behind you and put her feet on the back of your seat. Her
filthy sneakers are inches from your head and are touching the

brand-new coat you so carefully placed on the back of your seat. She's also constantly moving so that your chair is bouncing back and forth, leaving you nauseated and motion-sick.

The next time this happens to you, try the direct approach.

1. Sit up in your chair and turn around so you can see the offender.

2. Make eye contact and then ask her to please remove her feet from the back of your chair.

3. Tell her why: "You're getting my jacket dirty, you're inches away from my head, and you're rocking my seat back and forth."

4. If there is another empty seat nearby, point it out: "If you move a couple of seats down, there'll be no one in front of you, and we can both enjoy the movie."

The more confrontational approach:

1. Set down your popcorn, soda, or whatever else you may be holding. Give them to a companion or put them in the handy armrest refreshment holder.

2. Using either your left or right hand (whichever one is dominant), reach up as if you were raising your hand in class, but so your palm is facing backward.

3. Once your hand is fully raised so that your elbow is nearly touching your forehead, force your hand down so that you make contact with the feet resting on your chair.

4. Give them a good swat.

5. Repeat as necessary.

Smartphones and Other Electronic Offenders

Have you ever been to a courthouse or other government building where all phones, pagers, cameras, etc., had to be checked before you could enter? Perhaps this should be standard procedure at every movie theater, too, if the number of obnoxiously illuminated screens is any indication. But until Congress gets around to introducing that bill, you'll just have to deal with the situation in your own way.

See "Confronting Loud Eaters and Pesky Talkers," on page 170, for tips on how to effectively glare down your offender. If that approach fails, you may want to try moving seats. No good seats left in the theater? Try some more direct tactics.

1. If the offender happens to be easy to reach (i.e., if you're both in aisle seats or he's sitting in an empty row)—and if he doesn't look like a violent fellow—stand up and approach him.

2. Appeal to him by telling him exactly what the problem is: "Listen, your screen is really bright and it's hard not to see it out of the corner of my eye. I'm sure that's true of everyone sitting in your row and behind you. It'd be really considerate of you to put your [name of device here] away until the movie's over."

3. If that doesn't work, head out the door to find the theater's manager. That's right: tattle.

Concerts

There are as many different kinds of concerts as there are kinds of music: punk, soul, hip-hop, new soul, new wave, rap, classical, country, rockabilly, and folk. And each genre has its own, sometimes subtle, set of rules. At a country music concert, for example, it may be kosher for a cowboy to leave on his wide-brimmed hat even though it blocks the view of those standing behind him. But at a classical concert, keeping a hat on once you've been seated is positively taboo. And don't even try to start a mosh pit at a folk fest.

With these caveats in mind, here is a basic set of rules for concert attendees.

1.   No singing along with the soloist, whatever the type of concert (unless, of course, it's a sing-along).

2.   At a classical concert, refrain from clapping until the very end of the piece—not after each movement of the composition.

3.   Shouts of "Free Bird" should be limited to two.

4.   If you are tempted to flick your lighter and sway to a rock ballad, be certain your lighter is held suitably aloft so as not to risk lighting a fellow concertgoer's hair on fire.

5.   No inappropriate moshing.

6.   Remain in or in front of your seat no matter how enthralled you may be with the music. (This means no

impromptu air guitar solos or throwing oneself at the performer until after the performance.)

Moshing

In situations when a mosh pit is appropriate—at a Beastie Boys concert, for example—follow these moshing tips.

1. Stay relaxed and focused on the music. This will allow you to keep in your groove and move accordingly, as opposed to focusing on the people who are slamming into you (which may trigger some retaliatory instincts).

2. Though the proper term is slamdancing, bouncedancing more accurately describes the effect. The idea is to bounce off of others in the pit, not go at them like a bull rushing a matador.

3. If someone falls, be the first to rush to his or her aid. Help ensure no one is trampled amid all the fun.

4. If you're not enjoying the amount of physical contact in the pit, move to the edge, where you can still be part of the vibe but don't have to be physically involved. This tactic is always a good one if the other people in the pit

happen to be much larger than you.

5.   Do not violate the women in the pit by taking advantage of the close, unmonitored contact to make inappropriate grabs.

A Mosh Glossary

Slamdance: From the Latin slamdancus, meaning "dancing while completely caught up in the music." The general, all-encompassing term for what goes on in a mosh pit.

Stagediving and crowdsurfing: These enjoy a symbiotic relationship—one follows the other. After a fan makes it onstage and dives into the waiting pit of moshers, he is carried aloft and passed from hand to hand, thus crowdsurfing.

Thrash: An especially aggressive type of slamdancing that happens at skaterock shows, which range from punk to ska, funk to hip-hop. A little more acrobatic because of the physical talents of those involved: skaters, snowboarders, bike messengers, and the like.

Inappropriate Moshing

You're front row at a James Taylor concert. The legendary singer/songwriter breaks into "Steamroller"—which is, granted, one of his more spirited tunes. A fellow next to you becomes excited and butts his head into your arm. You enact a "polite fiction" strategy, pretending it never happened. But here he is, coming at you again. He's trying to create a mosh pit, starting with you.

Is this person someone's son who was dragged here but would rather be at a heavy metal concert? Or is he trying to subvert the folkie peace culture? Either way, he must be stopped.

1.   When you see him out of the corner of your eye, about to come at you again, take a step backward.

2.   He will miss contact with your body and butt into the person standing on the other side of you.

3.   Remain where you are to avoid further head-butting.

Stagediving

If moshing is what happens when fans get caught up in the music, stagediving is the culmination of a fan's fervor. It is completely understandable that a fan would want to (a) be close to the performers and (b) show his dedication to the band and his solidarity with its fans by initiating a dangerous maneuver in their presence. But, as with everything, there's a right way and a wrong way. Here are some rules.

1. Once onstage, be careful not to get in the way of any band members. Do not trip over electrical cords that may interrupt their playing or make you lose your balance and knock into a drum kit.

2. Limit your time onstage to 20 seconds or less to avoid getting nabbed by security. That means no extended antics onstage, no excessive showing off for the crowd.

3. Wear clothing devoid of hardware; remove piercings or spiked jewelry that could injure an audience member when you dive off the stage and into their arms.

Respecting the Performer

Out of courtesy to the performer, audience members should always refrain from heckling, throwing objects, and otherwise drowning out the music.

Invariably, however, there will be someone in your vicinity who just can't stop herself from singing along with every song. Wouldn't it be the same experience to stay at home, put on the CD, and sing along to that? Is she trying to prove that she knows all the words? Use the following approach to politely dissuade her from making an ass of herself—and annoying everyone around her.

1.   Turn to the person in question.

2.   Ask her please to stop singing, because you can't hear the singer you've paid to see: "Excuse me, I know it's tempting to sing along to everything. I love these songs, too. That's why I paid $65 to come here tonight. But I'd appreciate if you would stop singing so loudly, because you're drowning out the performer."

3.   If she continues to sing along, turn and glare at her, much as you would at a fellow movie patron who is talking too loudly. This glare should reinforce step 2.

4.   If she still persists, contact the venue manager and make your displeasure known.

Should this direct approach fail, move on to Plan B:

1.   Out-sing her. When she starts to sing, you start to sing, but louder and more obnoxiously.

2.   Make eye contact with her and begin to gesture and

dance in place as you sing.

3.   You may even try to harmonize with her—the worse you
      are, the better. Your horrendous singing will drown out
      her voice and make it futile for her to continue.

DINING OUT

The degree of pleasure to be enjoyed when dining out is de-
pendent on many human factors, including your companions
(who may chew too loudly and with their mouths open); the
waitstaff (who may be extremely rude and slow); and fellow
diners (who may eavesdrop on your private conversation).

One way to ensure an enjoyable evening on the town is
to prepare beforehand. Find out everything you can about the
restaurant in which you will be dining. Read up on it in guide
books or newspaper reviews, especially noting any comments
about the unusually rude or slow waitstaff. Visit the place beforehand during the hour you plan to dine to see how close
the tables are to one another and what the acoustics are like.

And when the time comes, observe these rules of good
dining behavior.

1.   Arrive 5 to 10 minutes early for your reservation.

2.   Observe the restaurant's dress code.

3.   Make sure you have the proper, accepted form of payment—if they don't take credit cards or checks, make sure you have enough cash to cover the bill.

4.   Do not try push ahead of people by bribing the hostess or haranguing her into giving you a table first.

5.   When ordering, try to limit the amount of special requests and substitutions. The items on the menu are the chef's creations and are made that way for a reason. (Of course, substitutions are fine if you're allergic to certain ingredients; if that's the case, explain it to your waiter.)

Once seated:

1.   Place your napkin on your lap.

2.   Turn off your cell phone.

3.   Do not reach. Instead, ask your dining companion to pass whatever you need.

4.   Refrain from placing your elbows on the table.

5. Recognize the limits of your language skills when ordering at an ethnic restaurant.

6. If you feel a piece of food stuck in your teeth, excuse yourself and go to the restroom to extract it. Do not fish around for it at the table.

7. If something is amiss, be polite about asking for it to be remedied. For example, if there's a spot on your glass or if you've been seated for a long time and haven't received bread or water, call over your server and explain the situation without assigning blame.

8. When you're finished eating, place your knife and fork squarely on the plate, the fork with the tines down and the knife with the serrated edge facing in.

9. After settling the bill, do not linger if other patrons are waiting for your table.

Observing Personal Space While Dining Out

Restaurants are public spaces, and the individual tables, booths, or banquettes become semiprivate spaces as soon as another individual or group is seated nearby, even if your space is demarcated by a potted plant or other divider. Accordingly, patrons must abide by a few basic rules of comportment when seated in a crowded dining establishment.

1. Keep your voice low and intimate; other patrons do not need to hear your latest political diatribe.

2. Remember the age-old rule about not discussing politics at dinner—even if you feel comfortable violating said rule among your own dining partners, others in the restaurant may not agree with your views. Try not to invite a confrontation.

3. Take care not to ram your chair against the chair or booth behind yours, especially while being seated or pushing away and rising from the table.

4. Similarly, make sure you keep your arms and legs within your own space. Don't stretch your arm out along the back of the booth so that your hand is hanging into the next booth, and do not lean your head back so that it's touching another person's.

5. Refrain from shouting to your waitperson from across

the room.

6.   Do not eavesdrop on other patrons. Even if you have
      nothing to say to your dining partner and you can't help
      but overhear another couple's conversation, do your best
      to focus elsewhere.

What to Do When the People Next to You Are Eavesdropping

Granted: Your conversation is fascinating, but that doesn't
mean it's acceptable for the couple nearby to be so blatantly
listening in. Not only are they not talking to each other,
they're actually tilting their heads toward your table, and occasionally one of them will react to your conversation with a
nod or a raised eyebrow.

The solution? Call them on it.

1.   Continue talking.

2.   When you get to the end of an anecdote or to a natural
      break in your conversation—a point when you would
      expect a response from your dining partner—turn to the
      eavesdroppers and ask, "And what do you think?"

If this less-than-subtle approach doesn't work, try to

have some fun with it. Filter some observations about your nosy neighbors into the conversation.

- Comment in general on people who eavesdrop: "Don't you think it's pathetic when people need to eavesdrop on other people's conversations because their own lives are so boring?"

- Introduce specific observations about the eavesdroppers: "Get a load of that guy's tie! No, don't look now, he's right behind our table. And his loser date! What a dog!"

The eavesdroppers should be hanging their heads in shame at having been found out—or perhaps they'll be so offended by your remarks that they'll ask to be moved to a different table.

Waitstaff Etiquette

If you've ever been a restaurant server, you know how thankless it can be—lousy tippers, picky eaters, and sore feet are all par for the course. With that said, it is a paying job, and waitstaff should provide at least a modicum of good service—which in turn nets a good tip.

You hold partial responsibility for the relationship—it's a two-way street, however short-lived your contact with your server may be. Here are some of your obligations.

1.   Treat your waitperson like a human being: make eye
     contact; be civil; do not look for ways to deliberately
     fluster him or her.

2.   Inquire about specials if these haven't yet been offered.

3.   Don't blame the messenger. If the kitchen happens to be
     out of your favorite entrée, it's not the waiter's fault.

4.   If your server appears to be falling down on the job (no
     water refills, longer than 20 minutes before serving ap-
     petizers or bread), politely motion him over to your
     table and ask why the service is so slow. Do not go to the
     manager unless the waiter is unmannerly during your at-
     tempt to resolve the issue.

5.   Good service deserves a good tip: Give 20 percent of
     your overall tab if the server went above and beyond;
     15 percent if he or she did the job sufficiently.

When the Waitstaff Is Rude to You

The waiter tosses your menus onto the table, barely makes
eye contact when he asks if you want anything to drink, and

responds with a grunt and an eye-roll when you ask for lemon in your Diet Coke. Is he having a bad day or is he rude all the time? Who can say, but if you stay at this table, your meal will not be pleasant.

Whether you like it or not, your waitperson has power. He and your food are alone together behind closed doors, and he can do things to it. Gross things. Your best approach is to recognize that power and not push his buttons.

1. Commiserate. Feel his pain. Call him by his name, if he offers it. Ask him how his day has been. Nod and say, "Uh-huh"—as if you've been there, too—when appropriate.

2. Don't be too demanding. Send your food back only if you cut into your meat and it's still raw or is simply inedible. When you do send it back, be apologetic about it.

3. If all else fails and your waiter continues to give you lousy service, approach the host or hostess and ask if you could be moved to a different table, one that's waited on by another server. If the host asks for an explanation, reply that your service has been unsatisfactory. In the interest of future patrons' satisfaction, this is information the restaurant's management needs to know.

When Your Date Is Rude to the Waitstaff

Everything seems to be going fine. Your date's on time, he's polite, he even brings you fresh strawberries, which is so much more creative than flowers—and better, because they're edible and you don't have to scavenge for a vase. Then you get to the restaurant and it's like he's metamorphosed from Dr. Jekyll into Mr. Hyde—he snaps at the valet driver and throws his keys at him. After you're seated at the restaurant, the waiter comes over to take your drink order and your date barks, "Pellegrino!" with not so much as a "please" or "thank you." How to deal with his blatantly rude behavior?

1.   You can start gently, with an observation: "So, you seem like such a nice guy, but I've noticed that you're not as easygoing when it comes to the waiter or the valet." He'll probably become defensive, and maybe a bit embarrassed.

2.   Follow up your observation with a request: "I'd appreciate if you could try to be more civil with the waiter. I don't want him to sneeze in our soup!" The joke will soften your reprimand and bring to light the possible consequences of his misbehavior.

3.   If you're certain that you don't want to see your date

again, apologize outright to the waiter for your companion's brusque behavior. After all, you don't want the waiter sneezing in your food. Mr. Hyde will likely be upset that you have undermined his "authority" (which he chooses to flaunt by being loud and obnoxious), but then you've already decided never to date him again. Continue to treat the waiter with kindness and respect.

Dealing with the Foreign Language Abuser

It can be highly embarrassing when a dinner companion insists on using his high-school French to speak to the waitress at a French restaurant (or Italian at an Italian restaurant, etc.). You've never even taken French, but you can just tell that his accent is horrific. "Ex-koo-say-moo," he says, "Newz voolonz oon puh de la waht-air." And the waitress, a French native, is trying as hard as she can to understand him. She smiles wanly and looks over to you pleadingly.

1. First, figure out what he is trying to say. It will be easier if he's speaking in a blend of French and English (Franglais), as in the example above. The poor man is obviously asking for water.

2. If he is not mixing English into his horrendous French, ask him point-blank what he wants.

3. Then explain your findings to the waitress. Do so lightly, so as not to offend your faux bilingual companion: "I believe he's asking for some rolls and ice water, please."

4. Suggest to your companion that he may want to invest in a three-day language immersion course to brush up on his high-school French.

ETIQUETTE TIP

Try mirroring your linguistically challenged companion to show him exactly how ridiculous he sounds. When he says something in his French, nod your head and respond. It doesn't matter if you truly know French—you may respond in English but with a heavy Pepé Le Pew accent, "Oui, oui, ma cherie, zee water ees so good." When he orders in "French," you do so as well, "I weel have zee cheeckEN wiz zee vegee-tables." Hopefully he'll get the point and realize that he's making a fool of himself (and hopefully the poor waitress won't spit in your soup for butchering her native language).

Dining Etiquette

Table manners are one of the oldest, most established areas of etiquette—they date back to seventeenth-century European social mores. Nowadays we don't use as many forks and aren't so stuffy; certain foods, like corn on the cob or crudités, are okay to eat with your hands. Nevertheless, there are still some basic rules of ingestion that we modern-day diners must adhere to.

1. Always chew with your mouth closed.

2. Do not try to speak while chewing.

3. Never make slurping sounds while eating.

4. When sharing food, it's best to cut a piece from the far end of the plate, place it on a clean plate, and hand it to your companion (unless of course it's a romantic dinner for two, where the food-sharing is foreplay and you couldn't care less about what germs your partner may be harboring).

5. Sip your beverage quietly, without gulping.

6. Refrain from belching or passing gas while seated at the table.

Foods You Can Eat with Your Hands

- Pizza
- Hot dogs/hamburgers/sandwiches
- Corn on the cob
- Unpeeled fruit
- Tacos/burritos/enchiladas
- Bread
- Chips and salsa
- Artichokes

Foods Commonly Mistaken for Foods You Can Eat with Your Hands

- Chicken drumsticks (Use a knife and fork.)
- Spare ribs (Ditto.)
- Shrimp cocktail (Use a cocktail fork.)
- Pastries (Use a pastry fork.)
- Lobster/crab (Pull out the meat with a lobster fork.)

Dealing with Sloppy Eaters

It could be a beloved relative or a colleague you hardly know. In either case, sloppy, loud eating is a habit that even the most patient and compassionate of us find difficult to endure. Imagine that you're trying to have a conversation with a friend but every time you look over at her, she has a food particle stuck to her face or tomato sauce dribbling down her chin. Maybe she's shoveling it in as if she hasn't eaten in a week or chewing with her mouth wide open. You can help, but you should be discreet so as not to hurt your companion's feelings.

1.   First, displace the blame. Pretend that she never received a napkin and call the waiter over: "Excuse me, could we have a napkin for my friend?" The fact that you think she never received a napkin may clue your dining companion in to the fact that she has food on her face or clothes. This self-awareness is the first step to recovery.

2.   If she's chewing while talking, feign concern over the amount of food that's actually making it down her throat: "Here I am making you do all the talking— you're not going to be able to eat your meal!"

3.   If she continues to talk and chew, cut her off and begin on a conversational tangent of your own, not letting her get a word in until she's finished chewing.

ETIQUETTE TIP

Another subtle way of telling your companion she has food stuck on her face is to hold up an object with a shiny, reflective surface so she can catch a glimpse of herself. It could be a new makeup compact you just have to show her. Or you can hold up your silverware for spot inspection and encourage her to do the same.

Dealing with the Nonreciprocating Food Taster

You're out to dinner with a friend and each of you orders something different. To be polite, you offer your companion a bite of your own meal, since it's so delicious and you'd like her to experience it, too. "Sure," she says, and you cut off a chunk for her. "Mmm," she says. "This is good." Then . . . nothing. She doesn't offer you anything from her plate. It's only fair that you get a bite of her food, since you just gave her some of yours. If she's not going to offer, go ahead and ask: "Can I try yours?" If she has any sense of propriety, she'll probably be abashed that she didn't offer in the first place.

Alternatively, after your companion has finished sampling your meal and hasn't asked if you want a taste of hers, just help yourself.

1.   With a smile on your face, so you appear nonthreatening, reach over with a fork and spear a bite, asking, "Do you mind?"

2.   Place your sampling onto your own plate, being careful not to drop it on the table.

3.   Chew slowly and appreciatively.

Paying the Bill

In some cases, it's clear who's going to pick up the dinner tab—for example, when just two people are dining and one has invited the other. Of course, the invitee should always offer to chip in; and when the invitee reaches toward her purse to pull out her wallet, the inviter should politely but firmly decline.

Other times, however, it's not so obvious. This little concern isn't really on diners' minds during the appetizers and entrées, but once those plates are cleared, the parties at opposite sides of the table begin to wonder, "What's going to happen when the check comes?" As soon as the waiter lays that leatherette folder on the tabletop, the dance ensues: "I'll get it." "No, I've got it." "No, let me." What are the rules?

1.   Etiquette experts advise that at a business dinner, the party who benefits most from the business association should pay the bill, even if that party did not extend the original invitation.

2.   If the benefits for both are relatively equal, the inviter should pay.

3.   If you're out with work colleagues for a business meal, the most senior employee should pick up the tab.

4.   Friends who are informally meeting up for a meal should split the bill. If one friend insists on paying, the other should concede but insist on paying the next time they dine together.

5.   The exception to the above rule is if one diner is much younger and less advanced in her career than the other diner, in which case the elder person should pay.

ETIQUETTE TIP
Should you be dining out with a friend who invariably—and very conveniently—"forgets" his wallet each time you meet up for a meal, be sure to give him a gentle reminder beforehand that you expect to be sharing the tab.

Laying the Groundwork Beforehand
If you're determined to pay, but you anticipate that the person you're dining with won't let you, there are a few tried and true ways to preempt an awkward situation.

1.   Arrive early for your reservation.

2.   When you approach the host to tell him you've arrived, let him know you want the waiter to hand you the bill at the end of the meal. Say, "Please make sure I get the check."

3.   Alternatively, give your credit card to the host before you're seated, letting him know that you'll sign the receipt on your way out. When you arrive at the end of the meal, you can inform your fellow diners that the bill's been taken care of.

Winning the Tug of War

With some people, the moment when the waiter slides the bill onto the table is like the first few seconds of a basketball game, when the ref drops the ball and the two centers fight for possession. You and your guest reach for the bill simultaneously, and each of you grabs an end tightly. Your eyes are locked and your foreheads are beginning to perspire. How do you win possession?

1.   If you're not already holding onto the bill folder with all your available fingers—for example, if you're only using your thumb and index finger—add the pressure of your remaining fingers. Holding on with all available digits will put you in a better position to twist the folder.

2.   Very suddenly, turn the bill folder from its horizontal
      position about 180 degrees toward the left so that your
      thumb is now underneath.

3.   This should be enough to loosen your companion's grip.
      Follow up this move with a quick tug toward your body
      to complete the maneuver.

ETIQUETTE TIP
Many diners abide by the "three time" rule. If physical
possession of the bill changes hands three complete turns,
the last person to hold the bill retains possession and
pays. Similarly, if one diner has said, "I insist on paying,"
three times, he retains possession and pays. In both cases,
it is incumbent on the other diner to graciously allow the
companion to pay.

At the Bar

When alcohol is good, it's very, very good. When it's bad,
things can get ugly. That's why it's important to be aware of
basic bar etiquette.

1.   Before you claim an empty bar stool, make sure no one is

sitting there. Although it may look unoccupied, people at bars are constantly moving around, so don't assume. Ask patrons nearby if the seat is free.

2.   Only one bar stool per customer.

3.   It's okay to ask a barfly to slide down for you if there are two empty bar stools on either side of him and you and your friend would like to sit.

4.   To get the bartender's attention at a crowded bar, squeeze between the bar stools, taking care not to jostle those seated around you, and then hold up some cash so he knows you need to order. If you see that others have been waiting longer than you, defer to them.

5.   If smoking is permitted, ask those around you if they mind your lighting up a cigarette, cigar, etc. Even if they acquiesce, try to exhale away from nonsmokers.

6.   If you knock over someone's drink by accident, offer to buy that person a fresh one.

7.   If there's no dance floor, there's no dance floor. Don't proclaim an area as the dance floor just because you

feel the need to boogie. Others may prefer to stand there and drink.

8.   Don't buy a drink for anyone without checking first to see if that person is accompanied by a date.

9.   Tip the bartender 10 to 15 percent of your bar bill—and at least $1 per drink. Leave more if it's an expensive mixed cocktail.

ETIQUETTE TIP

If you're getting up from the table to refresh your drink, ask your companions if you could get another drink for them as well; they'll soon return the favor.

Scanning and Scamming

It's no secret: people often go to bars to check out others who are single and looking for love. This may set the stage for all kinds of unfortunate situations, considering that (a) bars serve alcohol, thereby encouraging uninhibited behavior, not excluding approaching others and trying to pick them up, and (b) a lot of people do not find drunken strangers attractive.

How do you deal with someone who's decidedly not your type, but who's trying his hardest to pick you up?

1. Preempt the pick-up. From the moment you see him checking you out from across the bar, turn to avoid his gaze.

2. Stop yourself from looking over to see if he's still looking at you.

3. Don't even mention to your friends that you think someone across the bar is looking at you—they'll want to look over at him, which may give him the wrong idea.

4. Make yourself unapproachable by getting into an intense conversation with a friend.

5. Refuse any drinks he purchases for you. Even just taking a sip will invite him to spend more time glued to your side.

6. The first line of defense, should he make his move, is a simple, "No thanks, I'm not interested."

7. If that doesn't work, be firm and icy: "I'm sorry, but my friend and I are having a private conversation."

8. Should he be too far gone to get the gist of these not-so-subtle signs, be direct: "Listen, I'm flattered, but I'm not interested now and I never will be. Please, go away."

Defusing a Potential Bar Fight

The amount of alcohol imbibed directly affects the amount of time it takes for a trivial altercation to escalate into a full-blown bar fight: The more alcohol, the faster the fists come out. It's your responsibility to attempt to calm the situation before it gets out of hand.

1. Speak slowly and evenly while maintaining eye contact with an agitated bar-goer.

2. Address the altercation head-on: "Yes, I admit it. I bumped into your chair by accident. I had no intention of causing your friend's beer to spill all over her shirt."

3. Counter any foul language he may be using, or any names he is calling you—"mama's boy," "wimp," "klutzo"—with noninflammatory language.

4. Fight the urge to return the name-calling.

5. Introduce a solution to the problem: "Let me buy you and your girlfriend a round to make up for my clumsiness."

6. By taking responsibility for the situation, you will defuse his anger and, ideally, win his girlfriend's sympathy.

7.   Enlist her help in trying to calm her drunken boyfriend.

If he's too far gone and you can see that crazy glint in his eye, the best solution is to escape.

1.   If management is nearby, call on them immediately.

2.   If not, quickly look around for an easy escape route—a clear path to an exit. Make sure the doorway you've selected is not the entrance to the kitchen or the restroom, as entering these places would only trap you further.

3.   Once you've decided on an escape route, beat a hasty retreat, easing backward at first so that your eyes never leave those of your pursuer.

4.   Before he can figure out what's happening, turn and run from the bar as quickly as you can.

CHAPTER 7

While in Cyberspace

Remember way back when e-mail was a mysterious means of communication used only by the supertechies? Suddenly everyone had it. Then came texting—followed by the social media powerhouses, Facebook and Twitter, whose successes yielded the addition of social media components to pretty much every other website.

What does this mean for manners? With each new method of communication there are more opportunities for rudeness and newer ways for people to be impolite. Online, people can hide behind the mask of anonymity. Cyberspace is the new Wild West—a virtual free-for-all.

E-mail and Texting

The impersonal nature of communicating screen to screen aggravates society's already chronic insolence. When someone types a rude missive, or even just a few offensive sentence fragments linked by three-point ellipses, there's less of a perceived consequence for those actions. Yes, the words might sting the recipient, but the sender will likely not see the moment of impact and may never know the resulting reaction. Technology points us inward, and we lose sight of the effect we have on others—that is what it means to communicate in the twenty-first century. Fortunatley, there are guidelines that can save civility, against all odds.

Formality vs. Informality

E-mails and texts are typed, not handwritten. They appear on a screen instead of on a piece of creamy, heavy stationery. These are not good reasons to forgo the standard formats and pleasantries that have evolved over centuries of correspondence. And, just as handwritten communication varies in its degree of formality based on the scenario and the players, so should e-mail and texting. Here are some basic rules:

- The first back and forth with a person should include a

salutation ("Dear Jenna," or "Hi, Bob," etc.) and a proper closing ("Best, Rihanna"; "Sincerely, Dave"). Note: "Dear" is always acceptable and always correct. "Yo" is never correct and hardly ever acceptable.

- It's always best to err on the side of formality. If you've never corresponded with the person, and he or she is older, holds a higher degree or an advanced position than you, etc., always use Mr., Ms., Dr., etc. Take their cue. If they reply and sign-off as, simply, "John," you know it's okay to address them that way.

- Although emoticons and acronyms (LOL, OMG, etc.) can be handy tools for adding tone to a medium that often leads to miscommunication, most people are too heavy-handed with them. Never use either when corresponding about a business matter. Outside of business communiqué, use only sparingly.

- Never, ever sign off with "XO" (i.e., "kisses and hugs") unless you're writing to a family member or significant other.

Handling the Inappropriately Informal E-mailer

What if you're confronted with someone who is either unfamiliar or averse to these rules? It's your job to set the example. If the person is at all attuned to the social code, he or she will take the hint.

For example, say it's your task to welcome new members to an organization where you volunteer. You e-mail a new member, complete with "dear" and "sincerely" and full sentences in actual paragraphs structured with line breaks and other well-known punctuation devices. Your e-mail is countered with this one:

Hey, M! Thanks!!! Very psyched to be a part. xo

The signature at the bottom of the e-mail is a quote from Lady Gaga. Here's what to do.

1.   Forget the grammatical errors. Your task is to correct the level of informality. Do so by setting an example in your reply. Include a salutation and closing and write a message tinged with enough pointed shame to prompt the recipient to look back at her own missive and feel somewhat mortified:

     Dear Holly, Thank you for your prompt and exuberant reply. I'm happy that you're "psyched." Of course, the cause for all this excitement is the hard work that leads to the significant results we've been able to achieve. I look forward to rolling up my sleeves with you. Sincerely, Marcel

2. Should your recipient continue on her path of x'ing and o'ing, you could do ask her implicitly and breezily to please use your full name. Write something like, "Only my mother and my closest uncle are allowed to call me by a nickname." Take the edge off the remark with an emoticon, if you must.

3. If no adjustment is made in future e-mails you receive, you may want to pull aside the offending party at some point to explain that that particular style of communicating is not in the person's best interest. Presenting oneself in such a casual, almost flippant, manner does not command respect and will surely hinder future success.

ETIQUETTE TIP

Always let the older, more established, or senior-ranking person set the tone for e-mail correspondence. That goes for using nicknames, honorifics, and salutations—in short, whether your messages resemble professional, well-considered business memos or IMs between tweens.

Other E-mail and Texting Gaffes

There are so many ways for these correspondences to go wrong. Here are just a few points to be careful of while you're crafting a message and setting the tone for all virtual correspondence:

Flub: You send a long, thoughtful e-mail and get a sentence fragment in reply.

Fix: Manage your expectations. Most people e-mail via smartphones while shopping, talking, reading the newspaper, or worse. Only rarely should you waste your time on long, thoughtful e-mails.

Flub: You hit "Reply all" by mistake, sending a snarky message to the object of your snark.

Fix: Immediately send another message apologizing for your slip of hand and blame your bad attitude on the fact that you're having a bad day.

Flub: Others keep sending you typo-riddled and grammar-deficient e-mails.

Fix: All you can do is lead by example. Try using the same words they used, only spell them correctly and use them according to their proper definitions. Maybe they'll get the hint.

Flub: The autocorrection feature on your device turned something innocent into something pornographic, and off it went to your boss, religious leader, or mother-in-law.

Fix: An immediate e-mail correcting the autocorrected version, with a remark about how funny it was. Going forward, consider turning off the autocorrection function.

Flub: A professional business contact is texting you about meeting times and other work matters. As far as you're concerned, texting should be for friends and family. E-mail is for work.

Fix: Don't reply to the text. Instead, explain that you never use your cell phone and the best way to reach you is via your professional e-mail address.

Blogging and Online Forums

Blogging used to be special, but now it seems that everyone (and animals, too!) blogs about everything, from what they ate that day to how many times they meowed at the neighbor. Of course, some people's minutiae can be rather interesting and highly entertaining, even more so when their writing and Web design is top-notch. Quality aside, however, the problem with tell-all blogs is that the people about whom they're telling weren't asked for their permission. And then there are the nasty comments.

Blogging has a troublesome cousin in the form of online discussion forums, which pose as virtual communities and support groups but too often turn into battlefields for flaming wars. (Flaming is the act of sending or posting offensive messages over the Internet.) How should you navigate these murky waters? Here are some scenarios to mull over.

Blog Etiquette

The blogosphere is its own miniculture that runs parallel to our real lives. As such, it has its own rules that are often hard for a newbie to figure out. Here are some of the rules to follow for those who hope to evolve into respected and respectable bloggers:

- Only comment on another person's blog post if you're truly interested. Don't do it just to get your own link on their page, which is one form of "spamming."

- If you do comment, don't do so anonymously, especially if what you have to say is nasty. Doing so is both rude and cowardly. As a general rule, don't say anything in a comment that you wouldn't say to the person's face.

- Don't copy content from another blog and pass it off as

your own. Ask permission first and, at the very least, give credit to the original blogger on your site.

- Reveal relationships you have with the products, events, etc., that you are promoting. Full disclosure is the only fair policy.

The Ex Files

When Googling your ex-boyfriend, you discover some detailed tell-all posts on his blog about his ex, a librarian at the local law library named "Wren Jacobs." (Coincidentally, you're a librarian at the local law library named Jen Jacobs.) In these posts, he not only transcribes conversations and arguments—wrongly, so that he looks like the reasonable one—but writes explicit scenes straight out of a romance novel. You don't recognize them, although you seem to be the star of them. Or "Wren" is. How will you proceed?

1. Pick up the phone and call—don't e-mail—your troublesome ex. (If you e-mail, he could copy and paste the content into a blog post. Once someone starts telling all and begins to receive attention for it, there's no going back.)

2. Tell him you like his blog and think blogs are great, but

you noticed there's some material that somewhat resembles some of the stuff you did and said together. Allow him to answer.

3.   Let him know that everyone knows it's you and ask if he will erase the content that paints you in a negative light.

4.   Appeal to him by giving him some perspective. Say, "How would you feel if I was writing a blog with all sorts of personal information about you, and your boss and friends and family were reading it?" Don't let him get away with not answering this question.

5.   If he still denies his crime or refuses to remove the offensive material, inform him that you will start your own blog to set the record straight. Let him know you'll wait a few weeks to see if he comes to his senses.

Social (and Antisocial) Networking

It may be called "social" networking, but oftentimes that network feels like the playground you navigated as a child. Facebook and Twitter have us all agonizing over whom to friend and follow. As for those people who haven't joined these networks, they may be the smart ones. As you'll soon find out, once on these virtual playgrounds you're faced with plenty of potential for missteps. Here's how to maneuver your way among some of the sticky scenarios embedded in friend requests, tagging, defriending, and privacy settings.

Friending, Defriending, and Following

This activity is fraught with tension for naught. In general, friending and defriending go without notice. People are just too busy to watch whether their friend or follower lists have gone up or down a few ticks. Some rules:

1. If you receive an unwanted friend request, it's okay to ignore it. It's worse if you try to explain why you don't want to accept the request.

2. If someone brings up the unanswered request, be breezy: "Oh, I never check my Facebook profile."

3. When you defriend people, you need not notify them or anyone else. Just do so quietly, and they'll probably never notice.

4. Take a few minutes to figure out how to customize your privacy settings. You can preemptively make your profile invisible to other users. Or, if you prefer to hide in a more nuanced fashion, arrange your settings so that certain friend or groups are unable to see your updates.

5. Don't request to be a person's friend on Facebook unless you really know them. If you want to friend a friend's friend, include a personal note with your request, explaining how you know them.

Of course, there are plenty of hairy situations that have nothing to do with friending and defriending. Here are a few common ones, with advice for navigating them gracefully.

Flub: A married friend changes relationship status to "single" or "divorced," and the masses pile on, demanding to know what happened, or worse, if it's serious.
Fix: If this person is really your friend, call or at least send a personal e-mail. Don't add your voice to the rest of the nosy "friends." (And remember to hide your own relationship status so this public outing never happens to you.)

Flub: Your mom's on Facebook! And she comments or likes every single update, note, or photo you post. And her comments are kinda embarrassing.

Fix: Your mom has become your Facebook rash. You need to apply a salve—and fast. Let her know "the rules of Facebooking"—that you're only supposed to comment or like 1 out of every 10 updates, at most, that a person makes.

Flub: A Facebook friend's seemingly personal profile is being used primarily as a place to promote her business. Plus she's linked all her accounts—Facebook, Twitter, LinkedIn—so that each update to any account (or her blog!) appears in all three places. That means you're constantly hearing about her business when you're really only interested in updates on her kids and *American Idol* obsession.

Fix: Defriend and defollow. If she finds out and asks why, it's time for tough love. Say that her constant updates about her company from all three accounts were filling up your inbox, and you just had to take action.

ETIQUETTE TIP

Don't use any social networking account solely as a venue for self-promotion. Even if the page is explicitly for your company or business, your ratio of community-building to promoting should be about 80 to 20.

What and What Not to Post

When you stop to think about it, you find there's much more that shouldn't be posted on Facebook (or in other online forums) than should be. These "do not posts" range from things that make everyone else in your social networking universe feel uncomfortable to things that might get you arrested.

Yes:

- Insightful, funny observations about day-to-day life
- Links to articles or YouTube videos that will enrich or amuse the lives of others in your feed
- Vacation photos
- Announcements, whether minor (you found a store that sells your favorite European chocolate bar) or major (you just got engaged)

No:

- Granular info about sex lives or bowel movements
- Nasty passive-aggressive comments about your spouse or partner
- Tags of a person in a photo who is having a bad hair day or is engaged in or the subject of any form of embarrassing activity
- Photos of other people's children without their permission
- Anything private about anyone but yourself

- Photos from the delivery room
- How much you hate your boss or coworker

ETIQUETTE TIP

The beauty of social networking is how easy it is to disengage from someone who is offensive to you. You can hide their updates or simply defriend them. No confrontation is necessary, and no one's feelings are hurt.

Index